PITLOCHRY FESTIVAL THEATRE

PRESENTS

FAN FARE II

A COLLECTION OF RECIPES
FROM FRIENDS OF
PITLOCHRY FESTIVAL THEATRE
WITH AN INTRODUCTION BY THE
RIGHT HON THE EARL OF GOWRIE

ILLUSTRATED BY
MARGARET MITCHELL

SOLD IN AID OF
PITLOCHRY
FESTIVAL THEATRE

First published August 1985

Copyright 1985 © Pitlochry Festival Theatre

ISBN 0 9506349 1 3

Set in Souvenir, designed and printed by
The Allen Lithographic Co Ltd Kirkcaldy Scotland

CHAPTER HEADINGS

ACKNOWLEDGMENTS

I am truly indebted to everyone who has so cheerfully parted with their favourite recipes once again. I am especially grateful to HRH The Princess of Wales for her recipe. HRH The Prince of Wales formally opened our new Theatre building in 1981, and so the royal recipe ties in very well with that occasion. I am sorry that it has not been possible to thank everyone personally. I would like to take this opportunity to thank you all so much now, and those kind friends who have helped me so much in the preparation of the book. There has been no expense in preparing the book, as all have given their services free, including Margaret Mitchell (Maggie Thorburn) who has given so much of her time and skill in designing the front cover of the book, and the delightful illustrations inside – a very big thank you, Maggie. Also I would like to thank Mary Horsfall, Katrina and Colin Liddell, Elizabeth Dyer, Leslie McGlashan and Paul McLennan, for their help, and Annis Fulton and Jane Geldart for their typing, and also many thanks to The Allen Lithographic Company for their valuable help in the production of this book.

Barbara Liddell

Explanation of abbreviations used

Always read recipe first, and pre-heat oven when necessary before you start mixing.
Abbreviations used are:

tsp – Teaspoon
tblsp – Tablespoon
mins – Minutes
s and p – Salt and always freshly ground black pepper
dble – Double (for cream)
med – Medium
marg – Margarine

MINISTER FOR THE ARTS

When Barbara Liddell approached me to write a foreword to
the next collection of recipes put together by the
friends of the Pitlochry Festival Theatre I was delighted
and honoured to accept. Two of my great pleasures in
life are the theatre and food and both these have been
combined in this excellent and enjoyable book. I have
long been an admirer of the Pitlochry Festival and its
splendid Theatre, which must have one of the most
beautiful settings of any theatre in the world, and I
wish it every success in continuing its fine tradition of
regularly putting on a most exciting series of plays and
varied Festival events.

I know that "Fan Fare 1" was a great success and I am
sure the sequel will do as much to spread the good news
about Pitlochry, its Festival and its food.

The Right Hon The Earl of Gowrie
June 1985

We may live without poetry, music and art
We may live without conscience, and live without heart
We may live without friends, we may live without books
But civilised man cannot live without cooks.

American

Chapter 1

STARTERS & SOUPS
(hot and cold)

BAKED AVOCADO & PARSLEY BUTTER

2-3 avocados
1 tblsp chopped parsley
2 oz butter

2 tsp lemon juice
1 clove garlic crushed
s and p

Halve the avocados, peel and slice. Rub some butter over bottom of *le creusat* type gratin dish. Arrange the avocados in the dish. In a saucepan, melt the 2 ozs butter and add the lemon juice, and garlic. Pour over the avocados and sprinkle the parsley and seasonings over them. Cover the dish with silver foil and bake in a medium oven for 20 mins, Gas mark 4, 340°F, 170°C.

Prep. time: 10 mins
Cooking time: 20 mins
Serves 5-6

Jenny Abramsky
London

KIPPER CREAM

1 tin kipper fillets
lemon juice
s and p

½ pint single cream
6 eggs

Reserve 2 tblsp cream for the completed dish. Meanwhile, mash up fillets with rest of cream, season well and splash in some lemon juice. Divide mixture into 6 greased ramekin dishes and break an egg into each one. Top with spare cream, season with s and p and bake in mod oven, Gas mark 4, 340°F, 170°C, until eggs are nearly set. Serve with toast.

Prep time: 10 mins
Cooking time: 20 mins
Serves 6

Caroline Stroyan
Edinburgh

THE CHEDDAR GORGE

½ lb strong cheddar grated
¼ cream cheese
1 tblsp horseradish sauce

1 tsp mustard powder
2 tblsps sherry

Mix all the ingredients together and, if possible, blend in a mixer until smooth and light. Transfer to a dish and sprinkle with paprika. Delicious with biscuits but also makes a splendid Welsh Rarebit.

Prep time: 10 mins

Sue Wilson
Pitlochry

STRAWBERRY RISOTTO

2 ozs calf liver chopped in
  small pieces
4 oz Italian rice
1 small can strawberries (or
  ¼ lb fresh strawberries)
1 small rodichio (red cabbage)

1 clove garlic crushed
Parmesan cheese
white wine
s and p

Fry the liver and crushed garlic in a little butter till just done. Pour in a little white wine and simmer for 1 minute. Add the rodichio in leaves and fry for a further minute, stirring. Season to taste. Boil the rice till soft, drain, and add the drained strawberries. Stir the rice mixture into the liver and rodichio and put in the buttered ramekin dishes. Bake at Gas mark 3, 330°F, 165°C for 10 mins. Turn out and sprinkle liberally with Parmesan cheese – serve hot, decorate with rodichio leaves and strawberries.

Prep time: 5 mins
Cooking time: 30 mins
Serves 4

Amanda Dixon
London

EGG & CHEESE STARTER

Hard boil 9 large eggs. Stand in cold water and prepare **CHEESE SAUCE**

2 oz butter
1.5 oz flour
1 tsp dried mustard

¾ pint milk
6 oz grated cheese

Make white sauce with butter, flour, mustard and milk. Cool for 6 mins. Remove from heat and stir in half the cheese. Check seasoning. Chop the eggs. Place in shallow fireproof dish and cover with the sauce. Mix thoroughly and cover with the remaining cheese. Place under pre-heated grill until brown and bubbly. Sprinkle with chopped parsley and serve immediately.

Prep time: 10 mins
Cooking time: 20 mins
Serves 6

Countess of Strathmore
Glamis

EMERGENCY SOUFFLE

(Useful for that last minute panic when you realise you don't have a starter!)

3 eggs
4 oz cream, or sieved cottage
  cheese
1 oz chopped walnuts or similar
½ tsp cinnamon
1 dessertsp grated Parmesan or
  cheddar
mustard powder

1 bunch spring onions, chopped
  using all green bits or 1 onion
1 oz butter
¼ pint single cream
s and p

Fry onions in butter till just turning golden. Beat up all other ingredients well, except nuts. Mix in nuts and onions. Pour into greased ramekins and bake 20-25 mins in oven Gas mark 4, 340°F, 170°C. Serve immediately. You could vary the flavour by adding 2 tblsp chopped ham, or 4 oz cooked and peeled prawns etc, instead of the walnuts.

Editor's note: Souffles wait for no one, but a good tip, is to add a generous pinch of bicarbonate of soda, mixed in well, at the last moment before cooking. It prevents collapse, if guests are late – keep hot, but turn oven down.

Prep time: 10 mins
Cooking time: 20-25 mins
Serves 6

Susan Dixon
London

PRAWN FARCIE

½ pint shelled prawns
2 dessertsp parsley chopped
fresh breadcrumbs
black pepper

4 oz butter
2 cloves garlic, crushed
¼ pint white wine

Place the shelled prawns in 4 ramekin dishes, just cover with white wine. Mix garlic and parsley with softened butter and spread over the prawns. Dust with breadcrumbs and black pepper. Bake at Gas mark 5, 380°F, 190°C for 20 mins. Serve in ramekins with French bread.

Prep time: 5 mins
Cooking time: 20 mins
Serves 4

Amanda Dixon
London

PRAWNS IN WHITE WINE

1 pint prawns, peeled
2 shallots, finely chopped
1 clove garlic, crushed
1 tblsp chopped parsley

1 oz butter
1 glass white wine
2 tblsp cream
s and p

Melt butter in a heavy frying pan – add shallots and garlic, and fry gently. Add prawns and white wine. Cover and simmer for a few minutes. Add the seasonings and the cream. Bring to the boil, and serve hot with hot French bread.

Prep time: 5 mins
Cooking time: 15 mins
Serves 4

Jenny Abramsky
London

GAMBAS, OR KING PRAWNS FLAMBÉD IN BRANDY

allow 4 to 6 prawns per person
1 large shallot, finely chopped
1 oz butter
1 clove garlic, crushed

1 tblsp olive oil
½ tsp paprika
2 tblsp brandy

Melt butter in the oil in a heavy bottomed frying pan. Fry shallot and garlic gently for a few minutes. Add paprika and then the king prawns. Cover the pan, and toss the shellfish over a medium heat until their shells have turned a reddish brown. Add the brandy, and toss the shellfish in all the juices. When the juices bubble, serve straight from the pan. This is quite delicious, but very messy, so your guests will need individual finger bowls with warm water, and slices of lemon floating in them. We were given it in a lovely little restaurant in the Dordogne.

Prep time: 5 mins
Cooking time: 10 mins
Serves 2 or more

Jenny Abramsky
London

HADDOCK AND PRAWN SOUFFLES

4 oz haddock, when skinned
2 oz butter
2 egg yolks
¼ tsp anchovy essence
pepper

2 oz prawns
1 tsp lemon juice
1 tblsp water
3 egg whites

Very finely chop haddock and prawns. Melt butter and sauter fish quickly, mashing together. Stir in lemon juice, anchovy essence, flour and pepper to taste and cool slightly. Beat egg yolks with the water in a bowl over hot water, until slightly thick and creamy, add fish mixture to the yolks. Whisk whites stiffly and fold into fish mixture. Divide into individual dishes, placed in a roasting tin half full of hot water and put into oven at Gas mark 7, 425°F, 210°C for about 15 mins. Serve immediately.

Prep time: 15 mins
Cooking time: 15 mins
Serves 4

Ursula MacKenzie
Trinafour

HADDOCK AND PRAWN CRUMBLE

1½ lb haddock
1 small onion, chopped
½ lb cooked prawns
s and p
brown breadcrumbs
2 oz butter

1 pt milk
1 bay leaf
chopped parsley
grated cheese
2 oz flour

Cook haddock in milk with onions and bay leaf. Remove and flake fish, strain milk. Make a white sauce with milk from fish, and butter, flour and parsley (or parsley flakes). Add flaked haddock and prawns. Divide between 8 ramekins or scallop shells. Top with savoury crumble made with a mixture of brown breadcrumbs and grated cheese. Bake in oven, Gas mark 4, 350°F, 175°C, for 20-25 mins till browned and crisp. This makes a good main course dish – in which case cook in an ovenproof casserole dish and serve with vegetables.

Prep time: 20 mins
Cooking time: 20-25 mins
Serves 6-8

Janetta Watters
Strathtay

MUSHROOM DEVIL

2 oz butter
6 oz double cream
¾ tsp dry mustard
pinch nutmeg

1 lb mushrooms
1½ tblsp tomato ketchup
1½ tsp vinegar
s and p

Fry mushrooms in butter. Stir in everything else, and bake for 10 mins at Gas mark 7, 400°F, 205°C, in ramekin dishes.

Prep time: 5 mins
Cooking time: 10 mins
Serves 6

Clodagh Bonham-Carter
Comrie

ROASTED NUTS

2 cups nuts (peanuts or hazelnuts)
1 tblsp crushed rosemary
½ tsp crushed marjoram
¼ tsp cayenne pepper

1 tblsp melted butter or marg
½ tsp crushed thyme
1 garlic clove, crushed
salt to taste, roughly a teaspoonful

Melt butter, toss all ingredients in it, then spread out on flat baking tray and roast 15 mins in oven at Gas mark 4, 350°F, 175°C, stirring once.

Prep time: 10 mins
Cooking time: 15 mins

Elspeth Collins
Rannoch

MUSHROOM PATE

½ lb mushrooms
1 oz breadcrumbs
3 oz butter
nutmeg
a slug of brandy or sherry, optional

2 or 3 rashers bacon
4 oz Philadelphia cheese
1 small onion
a squeeze of lemon juice
oil
s and p

Grill bacon rashers till crisp. Drain, cool and chop. Soften sliced onion in oil, then add mushrooms and cook gently over low heat 2-3 mins. Stir in 1 oz breadcrumbs, cool. Liquidise this mixture with the bacon, cheese and butter, adding s and p and lemon juice to taste, and brandy or sherry if used. Leave for one day to mellow before using.

Prep time: 10 mins
Cooking time: 5 mins
Serves 6-8

Dinah Rorie
Laide

CREAM CHEESE AND CASHEW NUT PATE

8 oz cream cheese
1 pkt salted cashew
 nuts ground to a fine powder

1 tsp horseradish sauce
1 tsp paprika

Mix all the ingredients together and, if possible, blend in a mixer until smooth and light. Transfer to a dish and sprinkle with paprika. Tastes good spread on a rye or pumpernickel bread.

Prep time: 10 mins

Sue Wilson
Pitlochry

SMOKED SALMON PATE

(This can be made with kipper fillets, but poach in water first.)

6 oz smoked salmon (trimmings or slices)
s and p
1 tblsp dry white wine

¾ pint whipping cream
½ tblsp chopped parsley
1 tblsp whisky

Cut salmon into small pieces and place in liquidiser with rest of ingredients. Pour into small earthenware dishes and cover with clarified butter. Serve with oatcakes.

Prep time: 10 mins
Serves 4

Lawrence Healy
Edinburgh

SMOKED MACKEREL

First catch your mackerel. Loch Sunart ones are particularly fine! Cut a good fillet from each side (less bones that way). Place in earthenware crock, in the fridge – with dry salt between each layer, until you have a goodly number of fillets. Smoke the fillets in an Abu Smoker (obtainable from many fishing tackle shops). Served hot, they are delicious with horseradish sauce, or garnished with lemon.

Time: 30 mins   *Sir William Gray*
Serves 1 person per fish   *Salen*

SMOKED MACKEREL PATE I

1½ lbs skinned, boned and smoked mackerel   lemon juice
¾ lb butter   clarified butter
black pepper

Bought smoked mackerel may be used for this recipe (but only in extremis!). Place mackerel in the liquidiser with slightly melted butter. Add seasoning and lemon juice and blend together till smooth. Place in small pots and cover with a thin layer of clarified butter. Serve with hot toast as a starter or with salad as a main course. Will keep in fridge for several weeks.

Prep time: 20 mins   *Sir William Gray*
Serves: Starters for 16 people   *Salen*

SMOKED MACKEREL PATE II

1 smoked mackerel fillet
6 oz 'Piédou' creamed cheese

Mix together and season to taste in a food processor or liquidiser. A very quick and easy recipe for a last minute starter!

Time: seconds   *Rosemary Mackenzie Ross*
Serves 6-8   *Inveresk*

SARDINE PATE

1 tin sardines
3 hard boiled eggs
mayonnaise

dash Worcester sauce
pepper, salt and garlic salt (if liked)
enough milk, or top of milk, to
    make a creamy consistency

Place all ingredients in a food processor, and mix to a creamy paste, correcting seasoning to taste. Seal with melted butter, in ramekin dishes. Deep freezes well.

Prep time: 10 mins   *Meg Fergusson*
Serves 4   *Pitlochry*

PARTY HAM PATE (MICROWAVE)

1½ lbs lean ham
1-2 cloves garlic, crushed
4 eggs

1 large onion
1 oz parsley
1 level tsp sage
papper

Line a round, straight-sided glass or pottery dish of 7½" diameter and 3" deep with cling film. Mince ham until it is like a paste – then onion, garlic and parsley. Beat this with eggs, sage and pepper till smooth. Spoon into dish, cover with cling film and make 2 slits in it. Cook for 10 mins, rest 5 mins. Cook again for 10 mins, rest for 5 mins. Leave until cold. Serve with salad and hot buttered toast. As there are no breadcrumbs, this dish is good for slimmers!

Prep time: 5 mins
Cooking time: 30 mins   *Hazel Barbour*
Serves 12   *Fincastle*

AVOCADOS & MUSHROOMS
in a Mustard Sauce

2 avocados, sliced
2 tblsp olive oil
1 tsp parsley
s and p

½ lb mushrooms, sliced
1 tsp wine vinegar
1 tsp mustard

Arrange the slices of peeled avocados in a serving dish. Mix vinaigrette by starting with the mustard and wine vinegar, then adding the olive oil as if making mayonnaise. Toss the mushrooms in the vinaigrette. Add the parsley, and spread over the avocados so that the juice covers the whole dish. Season, and put in fridge for about ¾ hour.

Prep time: 1 hour   *Jenny Abramsky*
Serves 4-5   *London*

AVOCADO MOUSSE

2 or 3 large avocados   2 or 3 tblsp double cream
juice of 1 lemon   1 sachet gelatine
2-3 tblsp mayonnaise   s and p
(optional - 2 tblsp smoked salmon,
    cut into strips)

Mash the avocados, add lemon juice, mayonnaise and cream. Stir till smooth. Add seasonings – and, if you wish, the smoked salmon. Melt the gelatine in a tablespoon of water and add to the mixture. Make sure it is all well mixed. Grease a pudding basin or a loaf tin, or a mould, and pour in the mixture. Then cover it all up in silver foil, or the avocado will lose its green colour. Put into fridge for at least 4 hours. Turn out just before serving, and decorate with slices of cucumber and watercress. The trick is to make sure that the avocado does not discolour.

No cooking
Prep time: 15 mins   *Jenny Abramsky*
Serves 5-6   *London*

TUNA MOUSSE

7 oz tin tuna   1 pkt gelatine
cup chopped celery   3 tblsp lemon juice
cup chopped, skinned and   ¾ cup mayonnaise
    cored apples   one-third cup double cream

Sprinkle gelatine in ¼ cup cold water, dissolve over boiling water. Combine celery, apple, lemon juice, flaked tuna, mayonnaise, and season with salt and

paprika. Add dissolved gelatine to above mixture and stir well. Whip cream until stiff and fold into mixture. Spoon into mould which has been rinsed out with cold water. Chill well for several hours. Unmould and garnish with cucumber, tomatoes, avocado pears, etc. Serve with green salad.
This can be made with crab or lobster if preferred.

Prep time: 20 mins   *Jean Adams*
Serves 4-6   *Dalnaspidal*

EGG AND TUNA MOUSSE

1 tin tuna	rock salt
3 hard-boiled eggs	pepper
2 skinned tomatoes	chopped chives and parsley
½ tin condensed consomme	1 tsp anchovy sauce
2 small tsps gelatine	2 drops Worcester sauce
¼ pint cream	lemon juice to taste

Drain all oil from fish, flake it and put in bowl with chopped eggs and tomatoes. Add seasoning. The fish should not be mashed but left coarse cut. Heat consomme, add gelatine, allow to dissolve and cool. Whip cream slightly. Mix consomme into fish mixture, fold in cream, pour into souffle dish and refrigerate. Serve with toast. This also makes a good savoury.

Prep time: 40 mins   *Jean Rodger*
Serves 6   *Crieff*

CONSOMME MOUSSE

6 oz tin beef consomme	1 clove garlic, chopped
6 oz cream cheese	chopped chives to garnish
1 tsp curry powder	

Chill consommé in fridge. Omitting chives, put all ingredients in blender and mix till smooth. Pour into individual pots and chill for 1 hour or more. Serve with French bread, wholemeal bread or toast.

Prep time: 10 mins
Serves 4-5   *Jill Stroyan*
Double will fill 10 ramekins   *Killin*

ARBROATH SMOKIE MOUSSE

2 Arbroath smokies　　　　　　1 tsp gelatine
small tin evaporated milk　　　　1 tblsp cider

Remove fish from the skin, remove bones. Dissolve gelatine in a cup with the cider. Place this cup in pan of boiling water until thoroughly dissolved. Place all ingredients in liquidiser, and liquidise for a few seconds. Leave in fridge for an hour before using.

Prep time: 30 mins　　　　　　　　　　　　　　　　*Hazel Barbour*
Serves 4　　　　　　　　　　　　　　　　　　　　　*Pitlochry*

ARBROATH SMOKIES & AVOCADO PEARS

2 prs Arbroath smokies　　　　　lemon juice
2 large avocado pears　　　　　　olive oil
double cream, 4 or 5 tblsps　　　s and p and paprika

Remove meat from 2 pairs of Arbroath smokies, flake and pound in mortar, adding a little lemon juice, olive oil and seasoning until smooth. Put in a bowl. Pound flesh of 2 avocado pears and add to the smokies. Stir in 4 or 5 tblsps of double cream. Adjust seasoning, sprinkle with paprika and serve with toast or crisp bread.

Prep time: less than 30 mins　　　　　　　　　*Joan Kemp-Welch*
Serves 6　　　　　　　　　　　　　　　　　　　　　*London*

AUBERGINE SALAD

1 aubergine, approx. ½ lb　　　1 tomato·
1 med green pepper　　　　　　1 slice of onion
3 sprigs parsley　　　　　　　　juice of ½ lemon
3-4 tblsp Hellman's mayonnaise　salt to taste

Split the aubergine and green pepper in half, lengthwise. De-seed the pepper. Grill them both for 10 mins each side at quite high heat until softened. Squeeze them both in a sieve with a spoon, to remove as much moisture as possible and discard the skin of the aubergine. Place the solid left, in a food processor, skin the tomatoes and add with all the other ingredients, and process until everything is well chopped and a fairly smooth mixture is obtained. Chill for at least 2 hours Serve on a bed of chopped lettuce (or similar) with bread. Mushrooms can also be grilled and added as a variant.

Prep time: 20 mins, + 2 hours chilling   *Christos Bellos*
Serves 4   *Hersonnissos, Crete*

CONSOMME PETTIFER

tin(s) consomme (chilled)   mock caviar
double cream   fresh lemon

Whip the double cream. Put one dollop on each bowl of jellied consomme. Sprinkle the mock caviar on the cream. Hang a slice of fresh lemon on the rim of each bowl. Serve. It may not be cheap, but it tastes delicious, and it is not exactly time consuming.

Prep time: 4 mins   *Esther Rantzen*
                                                              London

PEARS IN TARRAGON CREAM DRESSING

3-4 pears (use ripe juicy pears   lettuce leaves (optional)
    such as comice)   paprika pepper (optional)

Tarragon Cream Dressing

1 egg   s and p
2 rounded tblsp castor sugar   ¼ pint double cream
3 tblsp tarragon vinegar

Method: prepare dressing

Break egg into bowl and beat with fork. Add sugar and gradually add vinegar. Stand bowl in pan of boiling water, stir the mixture until beginning to thicken then draw off heat and continue to stir. When mixture has consistency of thick cream, take basin out of pan and stir for a few seconds longer, season lightly and leave till cold. Partially whip cream and fold into dressing. Peel pears, cut in half and with teaspoon cut out core to stalk. Lay lettuce leaf on serving plate (breaking spine so that it lies flat). Place half pear in centre of each (rounded side up). Before serving, coat each pear with one tblsp of dressing. Shake a little paprika over top.

Prep time: 20 mins   *Colin Lamont*
Serves 6-8   *Glasgow*

QUAIL'S EGGS AUCHNAHYLE

1 doz quail's eggs
1 x 10.4 oz tin Campbell's
consommé condensed

lump of fish roe
sour cream

Hard boil eggs for 5 mins and peel. Put in individual ramekin dishes. Gently heat consomme and pour over eggs. Put in fridge to set. Before serving, top with sour cream, and lump of fish roe.

Prep time: 10 mins
Serves 6

Penny Howman
Pitlochry

SUMMER MELON

1 honeydew or 2 Ogen melons
12 oz mushrooms, cooked for
5 mins in 1 gill white wine

1.5 lbs tomatoes
½ pint well flavoured
French dressing

Scoop the flesh out of the melon, dice or make into balls. Peel, pip and quarter the tomatoes. Drain the cooked mushrooms. Mix the three ingredients in a large bowl and pour over the French dressing. Allow to stand for at least 2 hours before serving, stirring occasionally, it will make a good deal of delicious juice, so serve in soup bowls. Good with plenty of garlic bread.

Prep time: 30 mins
Serves 6-8

Sally Roy
Glenlyon

STILTON SWEET AND SAVOURY

6 ozs digestive biscuits, crushed
6 ozs soft brown sugar
3 ozs butter, melted
4 cloves
1½ lbs cooking apples, peeled,
cored and chopped

1 tsp demerara sugar
6 ozs stilton cheese, cut into cubes
1 tblsp port
4 fl ozs fresh double cream
walnuts

Mix biscuits with 3 oz of the sugar and the butter. Press onto the base and 4 cm (1½") up the sides of a 20 cm (8") loose bottomed cake tin. Bake Gas mark 4, 350°F, 175°C, for 30 mins. Cool, then chill in the fridge. Add the remaining soft brown sugar, cloves and a little water to the apple. Cook until tender, drain off juice and chill. Carefully remove biscuit base from tin, place on a serving dish. Fill with the apple mixture and sprinkle with demerara sugar. Place the stilton in a saucepan and warm very gently until soft but not runny. Allow to cool, then gradually add the port and cream, whisking till smooth. Place in a piping bag fitted with a large star nozzle and pipe rosettes on top of the apple. Decorate with walnuts and chill.

Prep time: 15 mins
Cooking time: 30 mins
Serves 6-8   *Christine Kinnear*
Definitely an extravagance!   *London*

SPINACH OR AVOCADO WITH PRAWNS

2 large pkts frozen spinach   2 tsp grated onion
1 pint aspic jelly   2 tsp Worcester sauce
½ pint mayonnaise   grated nutmeg
½ pint whipped cream

Defrost spinach, cook and cool. Add onion, Worcester sauce then aspic jelly, when cool, mayonnaise and finally cream and add nutmeg. Put into mould or souffle dish and put in fridge. *Decoration:* 1 lb prawns mixed in a French dressing with a few drops of tabasco or cayenne pepper. Instead of spinach this can be made with 4 ripe avocado pears.

Prep time: 35 mins
Cooking time: 10 mins   *Sue Sheriff*
Serves 8-10 helpings   *Ballinluig*

CAULIFLOWER SOUP

1 tblsp butter   2½ pints water
1 lb cauliflower   ½ pint milk
1 tblsp flour   paprika
s and p

Boil 2½ pints water and add level tblsp of salt, then add the cauliflower broken up into pieces, put lid on pan and boil for 10-15 mins. Melt the butter in another pan and blend in the flour. Slowly add the milk, stirring constantly. Pour in 1 pint of water from the cauliflower pan, then strain the cauliflower and add it to the milk mixture. When this boils it is ready for serving.

Prep time: 15 mins
Cooking time: 30 mins
Serves 6

Kate Douglas
Edinburgh

FISH CHOWDER

Smoked haddock, preferably Finnan, previously cooked in milk, boned and flaked. NB: retain fish stock.

1 large onion	fish stock from above
1 large tin sweetcorn, whizzed up in liquidiser	2 cups cooked peas
	bacon, fried crisp and roughly chopped
potatoes, steamed and cut into large dice	1 bay leaf
cream	butter
s and p	extra water if necessary

Chop onion, fry in butter and put in a casserole. Add fish, bacon, peas, creamed corn and bay leaf, and mix gently. Stir in fish stock. Add water if too thick. Season to taste. Heat up gently and add cream. The consistency of this dish should be quite thick. Serve with crisp warm bread. This is a very useful dish, as it can be prepared beforehand. Very warming and nourishing after coming in from cold outdoor activities.

Time: about 30 mins
Serves number of people according to
    amounts of fish and potatoes used

Sally Shillington
Louth

CREAMED ARTICHOKE SOUP

3 lb Jerusalem artichokes	chopped parsley
1½-2 pints chicken stock	1 egg yolk
4-6 tblsp whipped cream	nutmeg
s and p	

Scrub artichokes and drop into boiling water. Bring to boil, and boil 15-20 mins. Peel when cool enough to handle. Purée them. Add stock gradually, stirring with a wooden spoon. Bring to boil, stirring frequently. Remove from heat. Stir in beaten egg yolk and cream. Add seasonings and chopped parsley. Serve immediately.

Prep time: 45 mins
Cooking time: 15 mins
Serves 6

Elizabeth Soutar
Broughty Ferry

CONSOMME BORTSCH

whites of 2 eggs
½ lb minced gravy beef
1 large or 2 med beetroot (must
be round deep red variety)

1 quart well flavoured beef stock
s and p
soured cream

Whip egg whites to a froth, mix with the beef and put into an enamel pan. Peel and grate the beetroot, and add to the pan with the stock – whisk over the heat until boiling. Reduce heat, and simmer for 30-40 mins, taking care not to disturb the crust. Allow to cool slightly for 5 mins before straining through a scalded cloth. The consomme should be quite clear and a good red colour. Reheat carefully, and serve with a bowl of sour cream. A good party soup. To sour cream when none available, see recipe in Household Hints.

Prep time: 15 mins
Cooking time: 40 mins
Serves 4 good helpings

Rosamund Gruer
Edinburgh

POTAGE SOUBISE

2 pints stock (use Knorr beef stock
cubes for making this)
1¼ lbs onions
For liaison:
1 egg yolk
1 oz butter

2 oz flour
1 pint milk (hot)
2 oz butter

Cut the onions in slices and cook them for 5 mins in boiling water. Melt the butter in a large saucepan, and add the drained onions. Sauter them lightly until they just begin to colour. Sprinkle them with flour. Add the hot milk, salt and pepper to taste. Simmer for 20 mins, taking care that the soup does not stick. Put the soup in a liquidiser, or pass it through a sieve. Add the stock and simmer for another 20 mins. At the moment of serving pour the soup over a liaison of the yolk of egg and 20 gms (1 oz) butter.

Prep time: 5 mins
Cooking time: 50 mins   *Bill Rankin*
Serves 6   *Glenalmond*

SOMERSET SOUP

2 tblsp butter	2 skinned and halved shallots or
2 tblsp flour	1 small onion peeled and cut in quarters
1¼ pints milk	1 clove of garlic (optional)
½ pint cider	1 cup grated cheese (Dunlop or Cheddar)
s and p	
grated nutmeg	

Melt butter in a double saucepan, stir in flour and gradually add milk. Add onion or shallots and garlic if liked, and simmer over hot water for 20 mins. Strain to remove onions/shallots, return to boil. Stir in cider and cheese. Reheat but do not allow to reach boiling point. Season with s and p and grated nutmeg. This soup is very filling and warming on a cold day. To achieve a richer soup, thicken with the yolk of an egg or cream – but do not boil after either of these have been added.

Prep time: 5 mins
Cooking time: 20 mins   *Audrey and Jean Wright*
Serves 6   *Dunalastair*

LOVAGE SOUP

2 onions	2 pints chicken stock
3 oz butter	1 pint milk
6 tblsp chopped fresh lovage	s and p
leaves	lovage leaves and double cream
4 tblsp flour	to decorate

Sauter the chopped onion in butter until transparent. Add the lovage and cook gently for a minute or two before stirring in the flour. Cook for a few more minutes, stirring all the time. Add the stock and bring to the boil, stirring meanwhile, until the soup thickens. Cover and simmer until the lovage is tender. Liquidise the soup, add the milk and bring back to the boil. Season to taste. Serve with a fresh lovage leaf and swirl of cream in each bowl. *Ligusticum scoticum*, wild lovage, grows on Scottish cliffs. Grow *Ligusticum officinale* in the garden. It is a magnificent plant and can grow to at least 6 feet tall. It is perennial and seeds itself freely if allowed to. Lovage leaves freeze well. Package the chopped leaves in little bags with the amount clearly written on the side, as too much lovage will spoil the soup.

Prep time: 5 mins
Cooking time: 20-30 mins   *Peter and Marjorie Bourne*
Serves 6   *Aberfeldy*

PEA SOUP (HOT)

2 lb peas (fresh or frozen)   large bunch parsley
2 bunches spring onions   1 dessertsp sugar
leaves from large bunch of mint   2 tblsps cream
   (dried, or jelly mint can substitute)   4 ozs butter
3 pints chicken stock (water and cube will do) s and p

Put peas into a large saucepan and add spring onions (root trimmed). Add a large bunch of washed parsley, and the mint leaves. Add sugar and cream, and cover with stock. Simmer for 20 mins. Put through a mouli or liquidise, add butter and return to heat. Season with s and p.

Prep time: 10 mins
Cooking time: 20 mins   *Pat Bowden*
Serves a hungry 6   *Blair Atholl*

MINTED PEA & CUCUMBER SOUP

2½ pints chicken stock   1 pkt frozen peas ¾ lb
½ cucumber, peeled and seeded   2 egg yolks
2 tblsp butter   ¼ pint double cream
1 chicken stock cube for extra flavour   s and p
Chopped mint   sour cream for garnish

Simmer the peas in half the chicken stock, keeping the rest of the stock for later. Blend, when cooked, to a smooth purée in liquidiser, sieving again in wire sieve if necessary, to remove hard bits of pea skin. Cut cucumber into matchstick sized pieces and cook in butter till ready. Add first the pea purée to the remaining chicken stock, then the beaten yolks and cream, mixed together. Heat gently, being very careful not to allow to boil – add the finely chopped mint and the slithers of cucumber and serve at once with a blob of sour cream. If you are in a hurry, and don't have time to blend cream and yolks and to heat so carefully, add more peas and a little chopped onion. Blend the cream with a little cornflour and it won't matter if it does boil – and will thicken quite nicely.

Prep time: 10 mins
Cooking time: 10 mins   *Caroline Stoyan*
Serves 5-6   *Edinburgh*

ONION SOUP

2 cups milk	2 cups water
2 med sized potatoes	2 large onions
2 slightly rounded dessertsp oatmeal	1 stock cube
2 oz marg	s and p

Put liquid in pan. Roughly chop vegetables. Put veg and other ingredients in pan, and boil all together for about 1 hour. Leave till cool, and sieve or put in liquidiser. This makes a good creamy soup.

Prep time: 20 mins
Cooking time: 1 hour   *Janet Cameron*
Serves 4   *Blair Atholl*

STILTON SOUP

2 ozs butter	¼ pint dry white wine or cider
1 onion finely chopped	8 ozs Stilton cheese crumbled
2 stalks celery finely chopped	¼ pint single cream or milk
1 clove garlic finely chopped	freshly grated nutmeg
3 tblsp plain flour	Cayenne pepper, salt
1½ pints good chicken or veal stock	

Melt butter in a heavy pan and add onion, garlic and celery. Cook them on a low heat until onion is tender but not browned. Stir in the flour and cook for a minute or two before adding the stock, a little at a time to make a thin sauce. Simmer the soup for 15 mins, then stir in the wine and cheese. Stir on a low heat until the cheese has melted. Sieve or process the soup to a purée, then add the cream or milk and season it to taste with salt, cayenne and a pinch of freshly grated nutmeg.

Prep time: 30 mins
Cooking time: 30 mins   *Pamela Carmichael*
Serves 6   *Meigle*

PEANUT SOUP

½ lb peanuts   ¾ oz margarine
2 med sized onions   dash of whisky
1 pint chicken stock

Chop onions – soften in fat in pan over medium heat. Add finely crushed nuts and some of the chicken stock. Blend in liquidiser. Add more chicken stock to thin, salt and pepper to taste. Just before serving add a dash of whisky. NB: this soup thickens as it stands, so it is wise to have extra stock to hand. It can also be made with packeted roast peanuts.

Prep time: 5 mins
Cooking time: 10 mins   *Persis Aglen*
Serves 4   *Edinburgh*

CURRIED PARSNIP SOUP

3 oz butter   1 rounded tsp curry powder
1 lb parsnips   2 pints beef stock
1 med onion   ¼ pint cream
1 tblsp flour   chopped parsley or chives
1 clove garlic (if desired)   s and p

Chop up onions, parsnips and garlic, and slow cook in melted butter, with lid on for 5 mins. *They must not brown.* Add flour and curry powder, then gradually pour in the stock. Simmer for 20 mins – until parsnips are soft. Liquidise, add correct seasoning with s and p and more curry powder if necessary. Serve with parsley or chives to decorate.

Prep time: 10 mins
Cooking time: 25 mins   *Cecilia McLauchlan*
Serves 6-8   *Pitlochry*

PARSNIP CREAM SOUP

1 lb parsnips
1 pint chicken stock
½ pint cooked gooseberries or
  1 med sized tin
1 dessertsp honey if using fresh
  gooseberries
2 oz butter or enough oil to fry
  onions and parsnips

curry powder to taste
s and p
cream and chopped parsley for
  a garnish
1 clove garlic (optional) crushed

Fry chopped onions and garlic in melted butter or oil, till soft but not browned. Add chopped parsnips, chicken stock, s and p and cook until soft. Then add gooseberries and honey if used. Liquidise and add more liquid if too solid. Reheat adding curry powder to taste. When serving, add a dash of cream and a sprinkling of parsley to each serving. Can be made in advance for reheating on day of use.

Prep time: 10 mins
Cooking time: 30 mins
Serves 6-8

Meg Fergusson
Pitlochry

CREAM OF CHICKEN, AND/OR SPINACH SOUP

4 tblsp butter
4 ozs rice flour or plain flour
4 pints chicken stock or half milk and half water
½ pint cream
4 leeks (white part) or 2 onions if leeks not available

2 stalks celery
1 tblsp salt
1 boiling fowl
2 egg yolks

Heat butter in pan and mix in flour till golden brown. Add boiling chicken stock or milk/water, gradually. Add vegetables and fowl and simmer for 2 hours. Skim well. Remove fowl, rub veg through sieve, or put in blender. Bring liquid and veg mixture back to boil, mix half cream with egg yolks and add, stirring for a few minutes without allowing to boil. Finish with the remainder of cream. Correct seasoning. If soup is too thick, add more milk. Use fowl for another purpose.

Spinach Soup
Cook 1 lb of fresh well cleaned spinach for a few minutes with a little salt – no water required – when tender rub through fine sieve or put in blender. Then combine with the above chicken soup.

Prep time: 5 mins
Cooking time: 2¼ hours
Serves 6-8

Dorothy Stirton
Strathtummel

SENEGALESE SOUP

¼ cup butter
2 med onions chopped
3 stalks celery chopped
2 tblsp flour
1 tblsp curry powder

2 apples peeled and chopped
1 cup diced cooked chicken
4 pints chicken stock
1 bay leaf
1 cup light cream

Melt butter, add onions and celery and cook till limp. Add flour and curry powder, cook for 2 mins. Transfer to liquidiser, add apple, chicken and 1 cup stock. Blend until smooth. In a saucepan, combine this mixture with the rest of the stock, add bay leaf and bring to the boil. After a few minutes remove bay leaf and chill. Before serving cold, add the cream. This soup should be eaten very cold, topped with a sprig of fresh mint – but it is also very good hot. For freezing, put in containers before cream is added; this can be added later just before serving.

Prep time: 10 mins
Cooking time: 10 mins
Serves 6-8

Mary Horsfall
Kinloch Rannoch

SPINACH SOUP

4 oz butter
4 tblsp flour
1 chicken stock cube
1 cup single cream
s and p
nutmeg

2 small pkts chopped cooked frozen spinach,
   well drained
2 cups milk
2 tblsp sherry
1 small onion, studded with 3 cloves

Put butter, flour, 1 cup of milk, cream and spinach in blender for about 10 seconds. Place mixture in top of double boiler, heat over flame quickly, add stock cube and most of remaining milk. Stir over hot water until creamy. Add sherry and onion, simmer for 10 mins. If it seems too thick add a little more milk. Season with s and p and nutmeg. Remove onion and serve. Good hot or cold.

Time: 20 mins
Serves 4

Sally Roy
Glenlyon

WATERCRESS SOUP

1 oz butter   1 oz flour
1 pint chicken stock   2 bunches fresh watercress
½ pint single cream   (about 6 oz)

Melt butter, add flour and cook for a couple of minutes on a low heat, stirring gently. Slowly add warmed chicken stock until you have a creamy consistency. Wash the watercress thoroughly and add to the mixture. Cook slowly until the stalks are soft, stirring occasionally.
This will take about 20 mins. Remove from heat and allow to cool. Liquidise the soup or pass through a fine sieve. Chill and add the cream. Reserve a little of the cream to garnish the top of each portion. A few leaves of watercress, previously blanched, can provide additional garnish if desired.

Prep time: 2 mins
Cooking time: 25 mins
Serves 3   *HRH The Princess of Wales*

TOMATO DILL BISQUE

2 med onions, chopped
2 tblsp margarine
½ cup water and 1 chicken stock cube
   or ½ cup strong chicken stock
¾ tsp dried dill
150 ml mayonnaise

1 clove garlic, sliced
2 lb tomatoes, skinned and
   quartered
¼ tsp pepper
¼ tsp salt

Cook onions and garlic in margarine for 3 mins till soft. Add tomatoes, chicken stock, dill, salt and pepper, cover pan and simmer for 10 mins. Remove from heat and cool. Put through blender till smooth. Could be frozen at this point. If frozen take out 24 hours before required. Thaw, stir in mayonnaise, cover and chill overnight. Can be used as a starter but is excellent as a lunch dish served with crusty bread.

Prep time: 10 mins
Cooking time: 15 mins
Serves 6-8

Barbara Preston-Thomas
Pitlochry

CHEESE AND TOMATO SOUP

1 tin tomato soup
2 cups single cream
s and p

1 tsp lemon juice
½ cup cottage cream cheese
tabasco to taste

Mix soup, cream, lemon juice and tabasco. Beat until well blended. Stir in sieved cottage cream cheese, add salt and pepper, chill. Serve cold with chives sprinkled on top. This recipe tastes much better if made with fresh tomato purée instead of tinned soup. Can be made well in advance.

Prep time: 10 mins
Serves 4

Elizabeth Steuart-Fothringham
Murthly

ALMOND SOUP

4 ozs almonds, skinned
2-3 cloves garlic
1 dessertsp vinegar
1 large handful white grapes,
   peeled and stoned

2 tblsp oil
4 cups water
s and p

Mash 4 oz almonds in a pestle with 2-3 cloves garlic and 2 tblsp oil. Add salt to taste and 4 cups of water, added gradually. Or, mix all these ingredients very quickly in a blender. The result should look milky – chill thoroughly in fridge. Just before serving, add a dessertsp of vinegar. If you have a blender this is a wonderfully easy soup. The only chore is peeling and pipping the grapes, added at the last moment.

Prep time: 30 mins
Serves 4

Rosalind Stewart-Wilson
Moulin

AVOCADO SOUP

2 large ripe avocados
½ med onion
juice of 1 lemon
1 pint milk
1 pint chicken stock (cube)

tabasco sauce
salt
chives or parsley
prawns

Liquidise avocado flesh, onion and lemon while slowly adding milk and stock. Season with salt and a good shake of tabasco sauce. Keep in refrigerator until ready to serve. Pour into individual cups with a spoonful of prawns, and sprinkling of chives or parsley and a twist of lemon peel in the centre of each cup. This soup is a very attractive pale green colour, but turns brownish if exposed to the light for too long or if it is kept for more than 24 hours in the refrigerator. The contrast between smooth creamy avocado, sharp lemon juice and hot tabasco, is what makes this soup so delicious and it is therefore most important to taste it and adjust the balance carefully before serving. It may be served without the prawns with only a sprinkling of chives or parsley and a slice of lemon on top.

Prep time: 20 mins
Serves 6-8

Elizabeth Lyle
Dunkeld

We are told by J. Neil Leitch MD, MRCP, that: "Proper mastication greatly increases the amount of food assimilated, and also to a great extent eliminates indigestion. Eat thoroughly, thoughtfully and thankfully. We could do with a third less food if we would chew it *thoroughly*. To eat *thoughtfully* means to have a subconscious knowledge that you have chosen the right kind of food for your particular needs, and to eat *thankfully* is the bounden duty of us all."

Sent in by
Mary Rae
Aberfeldy

Chapter 2

FISH

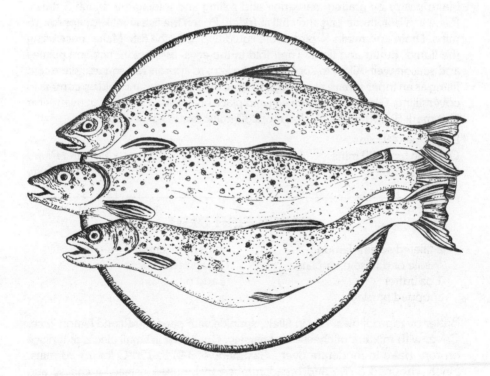

RUSSIAN FISH PIE

Filling

1 lb white fish fillet	¼ pint milk
1 oz long grain rice, cooked	1 oz butter
1 level tblsp flour	2 eggs, hard-boiled, chopped
4 oz onion, finely chopped	3 tblsp finely chopped parsley
s and p	pinch of mace

Pastry

5 oz firm margarine	7 oz plain flour
1 pinch salt	6 tblsp water
beaten egg to glaze	

Make pastry by grating margarine and rolling and folding the dough 3 times. Place in a polythene bag and chill in fridge. Poach the fish in milk for approx 15 mins. Drain and retain ¼ pint of the liquid and flake the fish. Make sauce using the liquid, butter and flour. Then fold in the eggs, fish, onion, rice and parsley and season well. Allow to cool. Roll out pastry to approx 12" square, place cold filling as an inner square at an angle to large pastry square, and fold up corners to cover filling. Glaze with beaten egg and place on a baking sheet, in an oven set at Gas mark 6, 400°F, 205°C, for about 30 mins. Serve hot or cold.

Prep time: 40 mins
Cooking time: 30 mins   *Margaret Rhind*
Serves 4   *Aberfeldy*

QUICK FISH DISH

2 filleted soles – lemon	juice of ½ lemon
sole or dab sole, or plaice	2 oz grated cheese
1 oz butter	s and p
chopped parsley	

Butter ovenproof dish. Lay in fillets, sprinkle with pepper, salt and lemon juice. Cover with mixture of cheese and parsley. Cut butter in small pieces and place on top. Bake in moderate oven, Gas mark 4, 340°F, 170°C for 15-20 mins. Finely chopped onion and breadcrumbs can be used instead of cheese and parsley.

Prep time: 5 mins
Cooking time: 20 mins   *Margaret Barbour*
Serves 2   *Fincastle*

CRUNCHY TOPPED FISH BAKE

4 plaice fillets or other flat fish
if preferred
4 oz grated cheese
1 tsp grated onion
dash of Worcester sauce

1 x 10 oz condensed mushroom soup
2 oz butter
crisps
dash of garlic salt (optional)
few anchovies (optional)

Lie fish in well greased ovenproof dish. Cover with the soup and top with cheese. In a saucepan, melt butter, add onion, Worcester sauce, garlic and crushed crisps. It is difficult to say how many crisps to use, but it should be approx 4 small bags. A little trial and error will get the exact quantities just right. Mix well together and spread evenly over fish. Bake at Gas mark 4, 350°F, 175°C, for 35 mins. This dish can be served as it is, or if preferred can be garnished with criss-crossed anchovy fillets. Note: no salt or pepper is necessary.

Prep time: 5 mins
Cooking time: 35 mins
Serves 4

Mary Horsfall
Kinloch Rannoch

FISH CASSEROLE

1 large onion
2 tomatoes
butter
2 oz mushrooms
¾ oz flour
2 tblsp grated cheese
chopped chives

1½ lbs white fish
2 tblsp chopped parsley
lemon juice
s and p
¼ pint cider
1 dessertsp fresh breadcrumbs

Peel onion and tomatoes, slice thinly with mushrooms. Put half prepared vegetables in bottom of a buttered casserole and arrange washed, skinned, de-boned and flaked fish on top, sprinkle with chopped parsley, lemon juice and s and p to taste. Cover with the rest of the vegetables. Pour over cider and dab with 1 oz butter. Cover dish and bake in a moderate hot oven at Gas mark 5, 375°F, 190°C, for ½ hour. Drain off juice, thicken with flour in a pan, and pour over fish. Sprinkle grated cheese on top, mixed with chopped chives and breadcrumbs. Brown under grill.

Prep time: 10 mins
Cooking time: 30 mins
Serves 4

Barbara Liddell
Pitlochry

FISH MAYONNAISE

1½ lb trout or salmon
4 hard-boiled eggs
cream or milk
s and p

mayonnaise
prawns
lemon juice

Poach the fish. Remove skin and bone and flake the fish. Mix fish with enough mayonnaise, single cream or milk, lemon juice and s and p, to taste, and to make a medium thick consistency. Liquidise the hard-boiled eggs, and put on the base of a serving dish, with the fish-mayonnaise mix on top, and garnish with prawns and parsley.

Prep time: 10-15 mins
Cooking time: 10 mins

Norah Douglas
Binbrook

BAKED TROUT

4 trout
1 tblsp water
juice of 1 lemon
s and p
chopped chives

chopped parsley
1 gill cream
few white breadcrumbs
margarine

Lay trout on well greased dish and add water, lemon juice, seasoning and good scattering of chives and parsley. Cook in oven for 10 mins, or till trout are cooked. Boil cream, pour over trout, powder with breadcrumbs, dot with margarine and brown under grill. Very quick and easy. Can be done with fish straight out of freezer, but then cook for longer.

Prep time: 5 mins
Cooking time: 15 mins
Serves 4

Mary Hamilton
Glencarse

QUICK BAKED TROUT

trout
salt
lemon juice

butter
hollandaise sauce

Clean trout and wash thoroughly. Line a baking dish with foil, lay trout on foil, sprinkle on salt and lemon juice to taste, add a few knobs of butter and bake in oven for 1-1½ hours, at Gas mark 3, 325°F, 160°C. Serve with hollandaise sauce, new potatoes and vegetables of your own choice.

Prep time: 5 mins
Cooking time: 1-1½ hours
Serves: depends on size of trout!

Ann Brown
Pitlochry

SALMON IN PUFF PASTRY

2½ lb tail end of salmon
s and p
beaten egg

2 large pkts puff pastry
butter

Skin and bone salmon, slitting fish into 2 pieces. Roll out pastry into a large rectangle. Place one piece of salmon in the middle – sprinkle with s and p and place the other piece on top, nose to tail, so as to make a regular outline. Sprinkle with more s and p, and spread soft butter over the salmon. Join up the pastry with beaten egg, cutting the corners first so as to avoid a bulky parcel. Place joint side down in a baking dish. Decorate the top with pastry leaves down the centre, making small slits between the leaves. Brush with egg and bake for ½ hour in hot oven at Gas mark 7, 400-425°F, 205°C and in a cooler oven at Gas mark 1, 275°F, 130°C for 10-15 mins, using own judgment. In Aga, cook for ½ hour in top oven and about 10 mins in bottom oven.

Prep time: 10 mins
Cooking time: 45 mins
Makes approx 12 portions

Lady Balfour of Burleigh
Brucefield

DISHWASHER FISH!

Wrap whole clean fish securely in foil. Put parcel in dishwasher. *No soap.* Run dishwasher through its full cycle. They say your fish will be cooked perfectly! Scared to try it?

Barbara Liddell
Pitlochry

SALMON PARCELS

1 salmon steak per person	s and p
butter	lemon juice
chopped parsley	

Butter both sides of salmon, and add chopped parsley, s and p and squeeze of lemon juice. Wrap each steak up separately in foil – roll up top and ends, leaving some room for expansion. Place parcels in a baking dish, and cook in oven at Gas mark 4, 350°F, 175°C, for 20 mins. Large fish may also be done this way, but allow 8 mins per lb plus 10 mins.

Prep time: 5 mins
Cooking time: 20 mins   *Catriona Godson*
Serves any number allowing 1 steak per person   *Chiddingfold*

BELL INN SMOKIES

4 small Arbroath smokies	pepper
8 fl oz double cream	¼ lb grated cheese
4 tomatoes	(Parmesan or Gruyere)

Skin the smokies, remove all bones and flake the flesh. Put half the cream in a buttered shallow earthenware dish. On this place the flaked fish. Blanch and skin the tomatoes and remove the seeds. Chop them roughly and spread over the fish. Season with pepper. Pour over the remaining cream. Sprinkle with cheese and bake at Gas mark 4, 350°F, 175°C, for 20 mins. Glaze briefly under a very hot grill. Individual ramekin dishes can be used instead of one large dish.

Prep time: 15 mins
Cooking time: 20 mins   *The Bell Inn*
Serves 4   *Aston Clinton*

FISH CURRY

1 onion, finely chopped
2 tblsp chopped parsley
1 tsp turmeric
½ oz desiccated coconut
½ tsp chilli powder
2 tomatoes, skinned and chopped
1 lb cod fillet or large haddock

2 cloves garlic, creamed
1½ oz butter
1½ tsp salt
1 tsp garam masala
    or 1 tsp curry or curry paste
1 tblsp lemon juice

Fry onion, garlic and parsley in butter in a 2 pint saucepan until it is transparent. Add turmeric, salt, coconut and garam masala (or curry powder) and chilli powder. Cook 5 mins and then add tomatoes. Cook until soft, add lemon juice and simmer 5 mins. Add raw fish cut into pieces 1"-2" square, cover and simmer 10 mins. Serve hot on rice with a ring of steamed courgettes or cook the courgettes in the curry, adding at same time as fish as they should still be a bit crisp.

Prep time: 15 mins
Cooking time: 30 mins
Serves 4

Margo Ross
Pitlochry

FINNAN HADDOCK WITH MUSTARD SAUCE

3 pieces Finnan haddock (2½ lbs)
½ gill water
2 cloves
1 oz butter
mustard to taste (moutarde de meaux)
chopped parsley

¾ pint milk
1 med onion, sliced
¼ bay leaf
rounded tblsp flour
s and p

Cut haddock pieces in half. Bring the milk, water, cloves, onion and bay leaf to a boil in a shallow pan. Put in haddock, skin side up and simmer for 10 mins. Lift fish on to a warm serving dish, cover and keep warm. Make a thickish sauce with butter, flour, and strained juice from fish. Lastly, add mustard to the sauce and adjust seasoning. Pour some over fish, sprinkle with parsley, and serve rest in a sauce boat.

Prep time: 5 mins
Cooking time: 20 mins
Serves 6

Margo Ross
Pitlochry

SMOKED FISH CASSEROLE

4 fillets smoked haddock or cod
2 heaped tblsp wholemeal flour
   (not too coarse)
about ¾ pint milk

4 large onions
3 oz margarine
s and p

Roughly chop onions, and lightly fry in marg, in creuset-type casserole. Stir in flour with a wooden spoon. Add milk gradually stirring well as in making a white sauce. Stop adding milk whilst it is still nice and thick, but definitely a sauce. Add a little s and p. Wash fish, feeling carefully with thumb to remove all bones. 15 mins before serving, bring sauce back to boil. Lay fish in casserole, covering each fillet with sauce. Cover with a lid and let it stand in a warm oven, Gas mark 2, 310°F, 150°C (very low heat, *do not boil*) for 10 mins. Serve with boiled potatoes, or macaroni. Vegetables or a salad are unnecessary with this dish. Its main charm is the sweet chunky underdone onion.

Prep time: 5 mins
Cooking time: 15 mins
Serves 4

Sheila Erdal
Ladybank

BELLA'S FISH CREAM

6 oz haddock (white)
1½ oz stale white breadcrumbs
s and p
2 eggs
2 oz butter

¼ pint milk
¼ pint cream
juice of ½ lemon
prawns or chopped parsley

Cook the haddock in the milk and 1 oz butter. When ready remove skin and bones and flake. Pour the hot milk mixture on to the breadcrumbs to soak, then add the fish, lemon juice and seasonings. Grease a Pyrex bowl, beat up the 2 eggs and add to fish mixture. Put into greased bowl, cover with greaseproof paper and foil and steam for ¾ hour, till firm enough to turn out. Using the remaining 1 oz butter, 1 oz flour, extra milk and cream, make a white sauce, adding prawns, or chopped parsley, and pour over fish cream. Serve immediately. This makes a good starter, or good lunch dish. It can be prepared early, to stage of adding beaten eggs, which should only be added just before steaming. It is also excellent made with smoked haddock.

Prep time: 5 mins
Cooking time: 1 hour
Serves 4-6

Rosemary Stroyan
Killin

BACON-STUFFED FRESH MACKEREL

4 fresh mackerel
6 oz streaky bacon, preferably sweet cured
dried sage

1 med onion
s and p

Clean fish and score the skin. Peel onion and mince finely with the bacon. Season with a very little salt but plenty of freshly ground black pepper and a good pinch of dried sage. Stuff mackerel with this mixture, reserving a little less than half. Press this into slits in mackerel skin and pile up any remaining over the fish. Place in greased ovenproof dish and bake at Gas mark 5, 375°F, 190°C, for about 30 mins. Serve with new potatoes and petit pois.

Prep time: 10 mins
Cooking time: 30 mins
Serves 4

Mary Horsfall
Kinloch Rannoch

SEAFOOD PASTA

1 large tin tuna fish
4 oz sweet corn (cooked)
1 clove garlic
1 large onion
herbs, lemon juice

1 lb shelled prawns (cooked)
4 oz peas (cooked)
1 tin Italian peeled tomatoes
1 red pepper
dry white wine

Chop the onion finely and allow to sweat over a low heat until softened. Add the tomatoes and turn the heat up to high. Add garlic, pepper and herbs (oregano or tarragon preferably) to taste. Finally add 2 tsps of castor sugar, turn down to low heat and simmer gently for 1 hour. When going dry, moisten with dry white wine. Chop up tuna into small chunks and mix in bowl with prawns, sweet corn, peas and some lemon juice. Allow onion and tomato mix to cool before mixing ingredients together. Fast boil pasta (preferably curly vermicelli), drain and pour cold water over. Drain again and baste in a mixture of butter and olive oil. Mix thoroughly in a large bowl with the seafood mixture and garnish with parsley and chives. Refrigerate well before serving – will keep for days. Above recipe for four can be easily doubled and trebled to make an ideal buffet dish for large parties.

Prep time: 1 hour
Cooking time: 1 hour
Serves 4 upwards

Leslie Lawton
London

RAW SPICED SALMON OR 'GRAVLAX'

2¼ lb salmon fillet   3 tblsp salt
3 tblsp sugar   pepper
fresh dill

Mix salt and sugar. Cut the fish into 2 equal pieces. Rub the salmon with the salt/sugar mixture. Place one piece of salmon in a dish, cover with a layer of dill and place second piece of salmon on top. Cover with silver foil and a heavy weight on top. Turn the fish twice a day for 3 days. Serve with creamed spinach and mustard sauce.

Time: 3 days   *Ingrid Wikstrom*
Serves 5-6   *Sweden*

QUICK TUNA CRISP
a good filling supper dish

4 oz short spaghetti   1 oz butter
½ pint milk   1 oz flour
1 onion (Spanish)   1 x 7 oz can tuna fish
3 oz grated cheese   1 pkt potato crisps
mustard, if liked   s and p

Cook spaghetti in water till soft. Make a white sauce with ½ pint milk in usual way, with butter and flour. Chop and sauter onion until transparent, but not brown – in a little butter. Add white sauce to cooked onion and grated cheese and season well. Add a little mustard if liked. Add flaked tuna and spaghetti and mix together carefully. Put into a 2-pint casserole and scatter crushed crisps on top. Bake at Gas mark 4, 350°F, 175°C, for 25 mins until brown.

Cooking time: 25 mins   *Ursula MacKenzie*
Serves 4-6   *Trinafour*

TUNA & MACARONI (MICROWAVE)

8 oz macaroni   1 pint boiling water
2 tsp salad oil   1 level tsp salt
2 oz butter or marg   2 level tsp cornflour
½ pint milk   3 oz grated cheddar cheese
1 onion, chopped   plus 1 oz grated cheddar for
½ red pepper, de-seeded and chopped   topping
1 x 8 oz tin tuna fish, drained and
   broken up

Place 1 oz butter in large deep glass or pottery dish to cook onion and pepper. Cover dish with cling film and pierce in two places. Cook for 2 mins. Add macaroni, boiling water, oil and salt, stir. Cook uncovered for 8-10 mins, until macaroni is plump and most of the water has been absorbed. Stir once or twice. Remove from oven and add rest of butter. Mix cornflour to a smooth paste with a little of the cold milk. Blend in rest of milk and pour over macaroni. Mix well. Return to oven and cook uncovered for 8 mins, stirring well after every 2 mins. Remove from oven and add 3 oz cheese. Stir well until melted. Sprinkle 1 oz grated cheese on top and add 1 tsp paprika if liked. Cook a further minute. Half turn dish after 30 seconds if oven has not got a turntable.

Prep time: 10 mins
Cooking time: 20 mins
Serves 4-6

Hazel Barbour
Fincastle

SALMON FRITTERS

½ lb cold boiled salmon
2 heaped tblsp flour
salt and cayenne pepper
Sauce:
4 oz melted butter
2 tsp flour
2 tsp mushroom ketchup

oil for frying
2 eggs
¼ pint cream (or top of milk)

2 tblsp cream
2 tsp soy sauce

Flake boned and skinned fish, and add flour, beaten eggs and enough milk or cream to make the mixture a soft consistency, like sponge dough. Season to taste. Have oil very hot, and drop in tblsps of mixture. Fry till golden brown on both sides. Drain on paper.

Sauce:
Mix cream with flour, and add to melted butter, heating and stirring all the time. When it has thickened slightly, add soy sauce and mushroom ketchup, mixing well.

Prep time and
    cooking time: 25-30 mins
Serves 3-4

Barbara Liddell
Pitlochry

ELEPHANT STEW

1 medium sized elephant
2 rabbits, optional

lots of brown gravy
s and p

Cut into bite-sized pieces, allowing 2 months to do this. Reserve the trunk to store pieces in. Add brown gravy to cover. Cook over charcoal for about 4 weeks, at Gas mark 9, 465°F, 100°C. Should serve about 3,800 people – if more are expected, 2 rabbits may be added. Do this only if necessary, as most people don't like to find hare in the stew. Good for a crowd.

Canadian

Chapter 3

MEAT – POULTRY – GAME

DINNER PARTY ROAST BEEF

You are having 8-12 people for dinner – and its to be roast beef.

You are serving cocktails, and cannot predict exact eating time.

So, at any hour of the day, from 9am to mid-afternoon, salt and pepper a 6-8 lb roast (prime rib, rolled sirloin etc), lard it with a piece of suet, and put into pre-heated oven at Gas mark 4, 350°F, 175°C, for 1 hour. Then turn off oven, *but do not open door*. Seal it, if necessary. when you prayerfully hope that the last cocktail is being served, go and turn on the oven at 350°F again for exactly ½ hour. This will ensure a perfectly rosy-rare roast. For medium rare – give it 45 mins.

Cooking time: 1½ hours   *Elsie Macnaughton*
Serves 8-10   *Pitlochry*

P.S. I have not had the courage to try this – but have come across this recipe before (Editor).

BEER STEAK

1 lb stewing steak, cut thin	4 large onions
1 can beer	sliced bread (brown or white)
2-3 oz margarine	s and p

Peel and slice onions into ¼" rings (roughly). Cut meat into pieces about 2" × 2". Brown meat in marg in frying pan. Then take out and keep warm. Fry onions till nicely coloured. Place in layers in a casserole dish, seasoning each layer with s and p. Pour some beer into the hot frying pan, and stir well to clean off all adhering meat and onion juices. Pour beer over meat and onions until just covered. Cut bread into pieces and place on top of meat to make a perfect 'lid'. The more perfect the fit, the better. Place in pre-heated oven at Gas mark 1, 300°F, 150°C, for 3 hours. The longer and slower the better. It should just make an audible bubbling sound. The meat is always tender and the bread absorbs the fat and becomes crispy, crunchy on top and soft and juicy underneath.

Prep time: 15 mins
Cooking time: 3 hours   *Sheila Erdal*
Serves 4   *Ladybank*

BEEF CASSEROLE WITH CHESTNUTS

3 lbs chuck steak
2 oz lard
15 oz can tomatoes
¼ pint hot water
¼ pint dry red wine
12 whole chestnuts (canned or fresh)

2 oz seasoned flour
1 med onion
4 oz canned red peppers
1 beef stock cube
3 oz sliced garlic sausage
butter

Cut meat into 2″ chunks, and toss in seasoned flour. Fry in lard until sealed. Put in casserole. Add chopped onion to frying pan, stir in any excess flour. Gradually add tomatoes and peppers. Mix water, stock cube and wine, and add to pan. Cut sausage into strips – add to beef and pour contents of frying pan over meat. Cook casserole in pre-heated oven at Gas mark 3, 320°F, 160°C, for 3 hours. Sauter 12 chestnuts in butter till browned, and add to casserole just before serving.

Prep time: 40 mins
Cooking time: 3 hours
Serves 8

Clive Perry
Birmingham

SAILOR'S BEEFSTEAK

3 lb potatoes
1 lb onions
s and p

1 lb beefsteak, sliced
1 bottle lager

Peel and cut potatoes in slices. Brown meat slices in hot fat on both sides. Keep warm. Fry sliced onions till lightly brown. Stir the frying pan with water or stock, reserve juices. Butter an ovenproof dish and start with a layer of potatoes, salt lightly, continue putting in layers, the onions, meat, potatoes and repeat until all are used, ending with a covering of potatoes. Put the juices from pan, and the lager, in the casserole, and cook in the oven on very low heat, for 2 hours. Gas mark ½, 280°F, 135°C. Serve with redcurrant jelly.

Prep time: 20 mins
Cooking time: 2 hours
Serves 6

Ingrid Wikstrom
Sweden

AUSTRALIAN BARBECUE MEAT LOAF

½ lb sausage meat   ½ lb minced steak
1 onion   ½ dessertsp chopped parsley
½ lb fresh breadcrumbs   ½ egg and ¼ cup milk
1 tsp curry powder   ¼ cup water
s and p

Barbecue Sauce:

¼ cup water   2 ozs brown sugar
¼ cup tomato purée   ½ tsp instant coffee
¼ cup Worcester sauce   ½ oz marg
1 tblsp vinegar   1 tblsp lemon juice

(Simmer this mixture for 5 mins.)

Combine all meat and dry ingredients. When thoroughly mixed, add milk and water last. When smooth, shape into a loaf with hands. Place on a greased roasting tin, and put in mod oven, Gas mark 4, 350°F, 175°C, for 30 mins. Remove from oven, and pour the barbecue sauce over the loaf. Return to oven and bake for a further 45 mins, basting loaf frequently with sauce. Serve hot, with veg, or cold, with salad.

Prep time: 10 mins
Cooking time: 30 mins   *Christina Kirk*
Serves 8-10   *Ballinluig*

STEAK FLAMBE

1 oz butter   2 tblsp brandy
1 shallot   ¼ double cream
¼ lb mushrooms   salt and freshly ground black pepper
2 slices fillet steak

Soften the shallot and mushrooms in the butter in a frying pan. When cooked but not brown remove and keep warm. Reheat the pan and fry the steak quickly. Return the mushrooms and shallot to the pan. Add the brandy and light. When the flames die add the cream and s and p and reheat. Serve immediately. If possible this should be done in front of your guests, as it looks quite impressive!

Prep and cooking time: 10 mins   *Ann Common*
                                                    Fortingall

AFRICAN STEW

2 lb stewing steak | ¼ tsp powdered cloves
2 large onions | ¼ tsp powdered ginger
2 large carrots | shake cayenne pepper
2 cloves garlic | seasoning
2 level tblsp tomato purée | scant tblsp lemon juice
1 bay leaf | ¾ pint stock or water plus 2 stock cubes
1 ½ oz butter

For liaison: 1 oz butter, 1 oz flour, 2-3 tblsp water.

Cut the meat into neat pieces, then peel and slice the onions and carrots and crush the cloves of garlic. Melt the butter in a large saucepan and toss the meat and vegetables in it for a few mins. Stir in the tomato purée, bay leaf, spices and seasoning, together with the lemon juice and stock. Transfer to a casserole and cook for 2-2½ hours in the centre of your oven at Gas mark 4, 350°F, 175°C. Make your liaison with the butter, flour and water. Add the liaison to the casserole, stirring well for a few mins until the gravy is well thickened. Taste and adjust seasoning if necessary. Serve with mashed potatoes.

Prep time: 25 mins
Cooking time: 2-2½ hours   *Bill Rankin*
Serves 6   *Glenalmond*

ITALIAN GOULASH

2½ lb stewing beef | 2 cloves garlic
1 lb fresh tomatoes or 1 tin | rosemary
6 tblsp white wine | oil
butter | s and p
1 tblsp paprika | stock

Cube meat and brown in butter and oil. Add crushed garlic and cook for a few mins. Add purée and chopped tomatoes (skinned if fresh), wine, rosemary, seasoning and a little stock. Bring to the boil and then cook in a casserole in a slow oven, Gas mark 1, 280°F, 135°C, for at least 2½ hours. Your can add small whole onions and mushrooms about ½ way through cooking time. This would be equally good cooked in a slow-cooker. Follow directions for stewing time etc from slow-cooker book.

Prep time: 25 mins
Cooking time: 2½ hours   *Peggy Watt*
Serves 6-8   *Glenfarg*

RICE AND BEEF CASSEROLE

6 tblsp oil
1 med onion
½ green pepper
8 oz can tomatoes
2 tsp salt
½ tsp chilli sauce
6 stuffed olives, sliced

1 lb minced beef
1 stick celery
7 oz patna rice
½ pint water
grind black pepper
½ tsp Worcester sauce

Heat half the oil and brown meat well. Remove meat and keep hot. Heat the rest of the oil, add chopped onion, celery and pepper and the rice. Cook until onion is lightly browned. Add tomatoes, water, s and p, sauces, beef and olives. Pour into an ovenproof casserole and cook in centre of oven, Gas mark 4, 370°F, 185°C, for one hour.

Prep time: 25 mins
Cooking time: 1 hour
Serves 6

Barbara Liddell
Pitlochry

ITALIAN BEEF CASSEROLE

4 lb should steak
2 oz butter
1 large onion, sliced
13½ oz can tomatoes
1 tsp mixed herbs

1 tblsp tomato purée
8 oz mushrooms, sliced
½ pint sour cream
2 tblsp sherry (optional)

Cut meat into strips and beat them until very thin. Then cut into small pieces about 1″ × 2″. Season with s and p. Heat butter in large pan and sauter onion in this until soft, add steak and continue to cook until lightly browned. Transfer to 4 pint casserole and add tomatoes, herbs and tomato purée. Cover and cook at Gas mark 4, 350°F, 175°C, for about 2 hours. Add mushrooms and cook for a further 15 mins. Remove from oven and stir in sour cream and sherry, then return to heat, but do not allow to boil. *If sour cream is not available, fresh cream will be all right, but it is not so tasty.* (See Household Hints for making cream sour.)

Prep time: 20 mins
Cooking time: 2¼ hours
Serves 8

Paddy Titterinton
Bankfoot

MINCE COLLOPS

1 lb beef, finely minced (from the rump) ½ small teacup water
1 tblsp flour   s and p

Put meat into a stewpan, and add a small teacup of cold water. Stir carefully until it comes to the boil. Season to taste. Pour into a bowl, cover with a plate, and steam for 1½ hours (over a pan of hot water). Then take it from the heat and add 1 tsp flour, mixed to a paste with cold water, and steam for another hour. A family recipe of 1880.

Time: 2½ hours   *Anne Howell*
Serves 4   *Pitlochry*

FILET OF BEEF BERCEAU (COLD)

1½ lb fillet of beef   2 pints well-flavoured aspic jelly
2 oz butter   6 oz liver pate
2 tblsp red wine

For garnish, chopped aspic jelly, watercress and radishes.

Aspic jelly: dissolve 2 oz of bought aspic. Powder in 1¾ pints of hot water, add ⅛ pint each of sherry and lemon juice.

Remove surplus fat from meat. Place in a baking tin, pour over the wine, and dot with butter. Cook in a pre-heated oven at Gas mark 3, 335°F, 165°C, allowing 45 mins, basing frequently. Remove, and leave until cold. Meanwhile, make aspic jelly, and pour about ¾" into the bottom of a 7" loaf tin. Allow to set. Cut the cold fillet into ¼" slices, and spread each slice with paté. Re-shape by pressing the pieces together again, and place in the prepared tin. Fill up with cool aspic jelly until the meat is covered. Leave to set. Put the remaining jelly into a dish. To turn out the fillet, dip the loaf tin in hot water and turn onto a wet serving dish. Chop the remaining jelly and place around the fillet, with watercress and radishes. Make day before required and refrigerate.

Prep time: 30 mins
Cooking time: 45 mins   *Rosamund Gruer*
Serves 6   *Edinburgh*

FRENCH MEAT LOAF

½ pint milk
3 cups (½ pint cup) soft breadcrumbs
1 tblsp Dijon mustard
1 tsp savoury (herb)
2 eggs, beaten

4 spring onions, finely chopped
2 tblsp chopped parsley
   (fresh if possible)
½ tsp salt
1 tsp thyme
2 lb minced beef

Soak breadcrumbs in milk for about 10 mins. Add spring onions, parsley, mustard, s and p, savoury, thyme and eggs. Mix thoroughly. Add meat and mix in well. Place mixture in a greased 8″ × 4″ loaf tin and pack down firmly. Bake in pre-heated oven at Gas mark 4, 350°F, 175°C, for 1 to 1½ hours. Serve hot or cold. To serve cold, wrap in tinfoil and place heavy weight on the meat loaf. Cool and then refrigerate for at least 12 hours before serving. This meat loaf is excellent, hot or cold, with baked potatoes. Will freeze well: keeping time, 2 months.

Prep time: 20 mins
Cooking time: 1-1½ hours
Serves 8-10

Barbara Preston-Thomas
Pitlochry

GLENURQUHART LAMB

1 to 2 lb breast of lamb, boned out
   or 1 loin of lamb
1 beaten egg
2 sprigs rosemary
s and p

1 pint breadcrumbs, brown
2 oranges
4 cloves garlic
6 x 8 cm pieces of string

Flatten meat on board, fat side down. Grate rind of orange, into crumbs – squeeze juice and add with seasoning and 1 crushed clove of garlic. Add egg until a soft consistency is formed. Spread evenly over meat and roll up. Tie firmly with pieces of string and place in roasting tin, with overlapping join underneath. Spear surface intermittently and plant sprigs of rosemary and slivers of garlic in meat – roast accordingly to size and family preference. Remove strings, place on an ashet and keep hot. Make gravy from juice and serve with rowan jelly or orange jelly (golden shred) or redcurrant jelly. Garnish with slices of orange and a bunch of rosemary.

Time: 20 mins plus cooking time
Serves depends on size of joint

Elizabeth Sandel
Kirkmichael

CREOLE ROAST LAMB

1 tblsp vinegar	½ pint stock
2 tblsp Worcester sauce	2 onions, grated
dash tabasco sauce	1 clove garlic
2 tblsp thyme, chopped	1 small leg of lamb
½ bay leaf	s and p
1 tsp browning	

Stir vinegar, Worcester sauce, browning, tabasco, thyme, bay leaf, s and p into hot stock. Add onions and garlic and cook for 5 mins. Rub the lamb with s and p and roast at Gas mark 6, 400°F, 205°C, for (20 mins per lb and 20 mins over), basting frequently with stock mixture. When lamb is cooked, slice what is required, arrange on a heated dish, drain fat from pan, and mix with any unused basting mixture. Reheat, season a little more if required and pour over sliced meat.

Prep time: 10 mins
Cooking time: 1½ hours   *Seonaid Hastie-Smith*
Serves 6-8   *Pitlochry*

GIGOT D'AGNEAU A LA FERMIERE

leg of lamb weighing about 3 lb	1 wineglass white wine
1 wineglass stock	½ lb each of new turnips,
1½ lb fresh green peas (weighed	and carrots
before shelling)	about 12 new potatoes
4 oz cream	2 oz butter
s and p	sugar

Melt butter in a thick pan, put in the meat and brown on all sides. Pour over wine and let it bubble a few moments, add the stock and cover the pan and place in pre-heated med oven, Gas mark 4, 370°F, 185°C, for 30 mins. Now add the carrots, turnips and potatoes, and 5 mins later, the peas. Season with s and p and a little sugar. Cook gently for 40 mins by which time the meat and veg should be ready. If not, cook for a bit longer. Pour off excess fat, sprinkle meat and veg with flour and add the boiling cream. Adjsut seasoning and simmer 10 mins longer. If mutton is used instead of lamb, cook for an hour at least before adding veg.

Prep time: 30 mins
Cooking time: 1½ hours   *Joan Knight*
Serves 5-6   *Perth*

SOMERSET HOT POT

4 lbs shoulder of lamb, cubed	2 oz flour (seasoned)
6 tblsp sunflower oil	2 oz butter
½ head of celery, sliced thinly	1 lb cooking apples, cored,
¾ lb onions, sliced thinly	peeled, cubed and sliced
1 pint light stock	½ pint med cider
1½ lb potatoes, peeled and sliced	s and p
rosemary and thyme	

Toss cubed lamb in seasoned flour, and brown in oil and butter. Drain lamb and put meat in a large casserole. Add onions to pan that meat was browned in and cook lightly. Add celery and apples, and sauter for a few mins, being careful not to overcook. Spoon veg over meat. Pour stock and cider over meat. Check seasoning, add more s and p if necessary and herbs. Top with sliced potato and dot with butter. Bake at Gas mark 4, 350°F, 175°C, for about 1½ hours until browned.

Prep time: 35 mins
Cooking time: 1¾ hours   *Ursula Mackenzie*
Serves 8   *Trinafour*

FAR I KAL (MUTTON AND CABBAGE)

This is a traditional Norwegian dish that housewives prepare in the Autumn, as soon as the slaughtering of sheep takes place. It is so easy to make, and is very tasty. It is even better the next day, so make enough for 2 days!

2-4 lb lamb or mutton shoulder,	1 oz butter
cut into suitable serving pieces	salt
(chops can be used)	1 tblsp peppercorns
4-8 lb winter white cabbage, or	flour
about twice the weight of meat used	

Prepare the cabbage by removing the thick stalk and discarding it. Cut the cabbages into rectangular chunks about 1" thick. Melt 1 oz butter in a large thick bottomed pan. Sprinkle with flour and place cabbage and meat in alternate layers. (Keep back some of the cabbage to add later, during cooking.) Sprinkle each layer with salt and a little flour and here and there the peppercorns. Pour on boiling water (or stock) until it reaches about ⅓ of the way up the contents of the pan. Simmer slowly 2-3 hours, stirring occasionally to prevent burning. It is better if all the cabbage is not added at the beginning but added at intervals throughout the cooking. Do be careful not to overcook.

Prep time: 30 mins
Cooking time: 2-3 hours   *Vivien Rossaak*
Serves 6-8   *Johannesburg*

LAMBS LIVER

½ lb fresh lambs liver
clove of garlic
sage

½ lb bacon
tomato purée
s and p

Chop the bacon into small pieces and place in frying pan, add the crushed garlic, fry till lightly browned. Remove from pan. Cut the liver into cube-shaped pieces, coat with seasoned flour (I often use wheatgerm). Fry quickly, adding 2 tblsp tomato purée, a sprinkling of sage, s and p. Add the bacon, mix and fry a bit more till suitably done. Very good served with mashed potato and salad.

Prep time: 10 mins
Cooking time: 20 mins
Serves 2 but can be doubled

Annabel Stormonth-Darling
Aberfeldy

PENNY'S KIDNEYS AND MUSHROOMS

4 oz mushrooms, sliced
1 med onion, chopped
12 oz lamb kidneys, cut in pieces
5 oz tinned tomato purée
2 tblsp sherry

2 carrots, chopped
4 oz bacon diced
½ oz flour
approx ⅓ pint stock
s and p

Sauter carrot gently in oil. Add onion, and when soft add bacon and kidneys and brown fairly fast. Add mushrooms and cook for 2 mins. Stir in flour and tomato purée. Add stock and stir till boiling. Simmer 15 mins. Add sherry and seasoning and simmer for 5 more mins. Serve with rice.

Time: 30 mins
Serves 2

Penny Howman
Pitlochry

PORC BRAISE AUX CHOUX

2 lb roasting pork
¼ lb streaky bacon (in a piece)
2 oz cooking fat
1 smallish cabbage

potatoes
parsley
s and p

If necessary, remove bone and crackling from the pork, and string it. Melt fat in a large pot and lightly fry diced bacon. Lightly brown the pork in this fat. Add seasonings, cover and put on a gentle heat. Divide cabbage into its separate leaves, wash and throw into boiling salted water. Let it boil for 15 mins, remove it from water, drain it and add it, with the parsley, to the pot containing the pork and bacon. Simmer, covered with tightly fitting lid, over a low heat for ¾ hour. Now add the potatoes, the quantity depending on the number of diners, replace lid and leave simmering for another ¾ hour. Remove the meat, remove the string and serve on a bed of the cabbage in an ashet or shallow dish with the potatoes in a cordon round it and the gravy poured over it.

This is a most succulent dish and I have found it to be a great favourite with my guests. Don't be put off by the instruction to boil the cabbage for 15 mins, which on the face of it seems far too long. Very economical on fuel – only one pot for meat and two veg.

Prep time: 30 mins
Cooking time: 1½ hours
Serves 6

Bill Rankin
Glenalmond

FILLETS OF PORK IN CREAM AND BRANDY SAUCE

1 fillet of pork
margarine
½ pint single cream

1 wineglass of brandy
s and p

Cut fillet of pork into small pieces and bash them out until very thin. Cook them gently for 3 mins on each side in good margarine, having added s and p. Remove temporarily and lay on one side. Add a wineglass full of brandy to the pan – reduce the brandy for about one minute, and add the single cream. Taste for seasoning. Replace the fillets in the frying pan, cover and leave on the side of a very cool stove to marinate until ready.

For a less rich dish, omit cream and use yoghourt. See Household Hints for stabilising yoghourt.

Prep time: 5 mins
Cooking time: 6 mins
Serves 6-8

The Marchioness of Aberdeen
Haddo House

PORK AND PIMENTOES

1½ lb pork fillet
2 oz butter
1 tblsp flour
4 tblsp cream cheese

4 tblsp corriander seeds and
 1 tsp black pepper, ground together
½ pint strong chicken stock
2 x 6 oz cans pimentoes

Slice pork fillet into ¼″ slices and beat flat, between sheets of greaseproof paper. Dust with ground coriander and pepper. Cook a few slices at a time in foaming hot butter. Transfer to a serving dish, cover and keep warm. Stir flour into juices and blend in the stock. When slightly thickened, add the pimentoes, cut into thin slices, and a little more coriander. When pimentoes are heated through, stir in the cream cheese. Check seasoning and pour over pork.

Prep time: 20 mins
Cooking time: 10-15 mins
Serves 6

Deirdre Scott
Farnham

PORK CHOPS WITH TOMATO AND RICE

A meal in one pot

6 pork chops	2 oz lard or dripping
2 med onions	1 small green pepper
6 oz patna rice	s and p
½ level tsp ground cinnamon	1 large tin tomato juice, made up
a sprig of thyme	to 1½ pints with stock
	1 lb small tomatoes

Fry chops briskly in fat to brown them. Meanwhile peel and slice the onions, slice the green pepper and wash out seeds. Transfer 3 chops to a large ovenproof casserole, sprinkle over half the rice, green pepper and onion and sprinkle with s and p and cinnamon. Add the rest of the chops and cover with the remaining rice, pepper and onion. Pour over the liquid and add the sprig of thyme. Put on the lid and cook in slow oven, Gas mark 2, 310°F, 150°C, for about 1½ hours. After 1 hour of cooking time, peel and add whole tomatoes. Remove thyme when dish is cooked. If the dish is to be reheated, more stock may be needed. Serve with a green salad.

Time: 1¾ hours
Serves 6

Molly Cunningham
Rannoch

PORK CHOPS WITH MUSHROOMS

4 pork chops with fat removed	8 oz sliced mushrooms
5 fl oz thick single cream	juice of 1 lemon
1 level tsp dried thyme	2 oz butter or margarine
1 tblsp plain flour	salt
freshly milled black pepper	

Thoroughly grease an ovenproof dish. In a frying pan brown chops well on both sides and transfer to ovenproof dish. Season each one with salt, pepper and the thyme. Fry sliced mushrooms in the same pan, pour lemon juice ovr and allow to bubble for a moment before adding the flour. Spoon mixture over the chops. Spoon the cream over the chops and cover tightly with foil. Bake for 1 hour at Gas mark 4, 350°F, 175°C, and serve with broccoli and mashed potatoes.

Prep time: 10 mins
Cooking time: 1 hour
Serves 4

Mary Horsfall
Kinloch Rannoch

PONCHITOS

4 very thin slices boned leg of pork
　or 1½ pork fillets, sliced thinly
3 cloves garlic
½ tsp ground cinnamon
red wine
1 large red pepper

a large bunch of fresh oregano
　or marjoram, or heaped
　tsp dried cumin
olive oil
s and p

Put everything except the meat, oil and wine into the blender. Liquidise and add a splash of red wine and about ¼ pint or less of oil – enough to make a fairly runny sauce. Pour over slices of pork and leave to marinate in fridge for at least 30 mins. Grill the pork, basting occasionally with sauce, until cooked. Alternatively, this makes an excellent barbeque dish. Recipe from a bar in Spain.

Prep time: 10 mins plus
Cooking time: 10 mins
Serves 4

Henrietta Thewes
Killiecrankie

BARBECUED SPARE RIBS

¼ cup oil
1 tsp garlic, crushed
2 med onions, finely chopped
1 tsp basil or thyme
½ cup beef stock
1 tsp dry mustard

12½ oz can tomato purée
¼ cup white vinegar
1 tsp salt
¼ cup honey
½ cup Worcester sauce
4 lb spare ribs

Heat the oil in a 10″ or 12″ frying pan – add the garlic and onions and cook stirring frequently for 3-4 mins without letting onions brown. Combine the tomato paste and vinegar, then add to the frying pan, stir in the salt, basil or thyme, honey and beef stock, Worcester sauce and mustard. Mix thoroughly, simmer uncovered over low heat 10-15 mins. Remove from heat, pre-heat oven to Gas mark 7, 400°F, 205°C. Place spare ribs fat side up on a rack set in a shallow roasting pan, and with a pastry brush thoroughly coat surface of meat with the sauce. Bake in middle of oven for 45 mins to 1 hour, basting thoroughly with sauce every 10 mins or so. When spare ribs are brown and crisp, cut into individual portions and serve at once with salads and rice. Youngsters enjoy it – no knives or forks required for spare ribs.

Prep time: 25-30 mins (Sauce)
Cooking time: ¾ to 1 hour   *Helen Benzies*
Serves 4-6   *Meigle*

SAUSAGE PLAIT

1 lb sausage meat	2 med sized onions
1 lb plain flour	pinch salt
8 oz fat	water
mixed herbs (optional)	1 egg, beaten

Sieve flour into bowl with salt. Rub in fat until breadcrumb texture. Add sufficient water until a stiff dough is reached. Roll out dough on a floured surface to a size of 10″ × 12″. To make filling, put sausage meat, and sliced onions and mixed herbs to taste with some of the beaten egg in a bowl and mix well. (Keep some of the beaten egg aside to glaze top of pastry later.) Roll sausage meat mixture into a tube, the length of the pastry, lay it in the centre of the pastry. To get the plait effect, slice pastry either side diagonally, and then criss cross alternate slices of pastry from left and right until all have been used. Glaze with rest of egg and bake at Gas mark 6, 380°F, 195°C, for 40-50 mins.

Prep time: 20 mins
Cooking time: 40-50 mins   *Karen Robinson*
Serves 6   *Eastleigh*

SWEDISH DREAM HAM

14 fl oz cream	12 slices boiled ham
sherry	2 tblsp tomato purée or chilli sauce
1 tsp curry powder	butter

Soak the ham slices in the sherry, and leave for a couple of hours or longer if you wish. Butter a shallow fireproof dish and arrange the slices in it. Then mix the cream (not whipped) with the tomato purée or chilli sauce, and curry powder.

Pour the cream mixture over the ham, dot with butter and bake in the oven at Gas mark 6, 390°F, 200°C, for 30-35 mins. Serve with rice.

Prep time: 2 hours marinading
Cooking time: 30-35 mins
Serves 5-6

Ingrid Wikstrom
Sweden

A similar recipe, substituting 8 oz mushrooms, a drained can of pimentoes, 2 or 3 dessertsp chilli sauce, and grated cheese, for tomato purée and curry powder, was also sent in.

Catriona Godson
Chiddingfold

DRAMBUIE BRAISED HAM

Sliced cooked gammon or gammon
   steaks, as per your numbers
orange juice, fresh or tinned

a few cloves
brown sugar
Drambuie to taste

Place ham in ovenproof serving dish – cover with orange juice, add cloves and sugar and cover. Bake 40 mins or so in medium oven, Gas mark 4, 370°F, 185°C. Pour over Drambuie to taste, just before serving. Garnish with slices of orange and watercress (if available) or parsley.

Prep time: 5 mins
Cooking time: 40 mins
Serves as many as you cater for

Elizabeth Sandel
Kirkmichael

HONEYED GRAPEFRUIT CHICKEN

3-4 lb chicken
2 tblsp double cream
1 tblsp honey
green olives for garnish
s and p

2 small grapefruit and the rind of one of them
1 glass white wine
1 tsp ginger
a little fresh tarragon
crushed garlic to taste (optional)

Put chicken in a roasting tin and rub ginger and seasoning all over the breast. Peel one grapefruit after grating rind from it, reserve rind. Stuff the chicken with half the segments and the tarragon. Also the crushed garlic if liked. Cut the other grapefruit in half and pour juice over chicken. Cook in a fairly hot oven, Gas mark 5-6, 370-400°F, 185-205°C, for ¾ hour. Then remove and spoon the honey over the chicken. Add the white wine, and baste. Sprinkle some of the grated grapefruit rind into the dish and put back into the oven for a further ½ to ¾ hour, depending on the size of the chicken. When cooked, place chicken on a serving dish and keep hot – pour off the excess fat, stir in the cream and serve with the chicken. Garnish the chicken with the rest of the grapefruit segments and grated rind, and add a few green olives.

Prep time: 15 mins
Cooking time: 1½ hours
Serves 4-6

Joan Knight
Perth

LEMON CHICKEN WITH ALMONDS

4 chicken pieces	4 oz onion sliced
¼ pint sherry	3 oz butter
1 tblsp lemon juice	finely grated rind 1 lemon
¼ level tsp cinnamon	¼ level tsp ginger
¼ pint stock	¼ pint single cream
s and p	1 oz toasted flaked almonds
chopped parsley	

Marinate chicken in onion and sherry for 2 hours. Cream butter, beat in lemon juice and rind, cinnamon and ginger, and spread over chicken. Place pieces on a bed of onions in a casserole dish. Spoon marinade over and roast at Gas mark 9, 500°F, 250°C, 15 mins. Reduce to Gas mark 4, 370°F, 180°C, for ¾ hour. Remove chicken and keep warm. Add stock to casserole and thicken if preferred. Add cream, replace chicken, and sprinkle with almonds and parsley.

Prep time: 2 hours marinating time
Cooking time: 1 hour
Serves 4

Penny Howman
Pitlochry

POULET NAVARRAIS

1 chicken weighing 2 lb 4 oz	2 oz butter
12 dessertsp madeira	½ lb mushrooms
2 oz tomato purée	1½ oz cornflour

Cut the chicken up into the usual joints. Heat the butter in a large pan and add the chicken portions. Sauter them until they are golden. Pour in the maderia, and season to taste. Add the tomato purée and the mushrooms, which have been washed, peeled and sliced. Cover the pot with greaseproof paper before putting on the lid, to seal the pot as hermetically as possible. Leave it to cook gently for

45 mins. Remove the chicken portions to a heated serving dish. Make a liaison with the cornflour. Check the seasoning and cover the chicken portions with sauce.

Prep time: 10 mins
Cooking time: 65 mins　　　　　　　　　　　　　　*Bill Rankin*
Serves 4-6　　　　　　　　　　　　　　　　　　*Glenalmond*

CHICKEN ROULADE WITH BACON AND MUSHROOMS

1½ oz butter
4 oz button mushrooms, chopped
1 oz plain flour
8 oz cooked chicken, finely diced
1 tsp dried tarragon
pinch nutmeg

4 oz bacon, derinded and chopped
¾ pint milk
½ oz cornflour
4 eggs, separated
s and p
1 oz cheddar cheese, grated

Line an 8″ × 12″ Swiss roll tin with oiled greaseproof paper. Melt butter. Add bacon and mushrooms and fry for 3-4 mins. Remove from pan with slotted spoon and set aside. Stir flour into remaining butter in pan and cook for 2-3 mins. Remove from heat. Blend the cornflour with the milk and stir into pan, mixing well. Bring the sauce to the boil and simmer for 2-3 mins. Put the diced chicken into a large bowl and stir in 3 tblsp of the sauce. Beat the egg yolks one at a time into this mixture, adding the tarragon, s and p. Stiffly whisk egg whites and fold into chicken mixture. Spoon on to prepared tin and smooth out. Bake in preheated oven at Gas mark 6, 400°F, 205°C, for 10-15 mins until set and golden brown. Meanwhile stir bacon and mushrooms into remaining sauce, with s and p and nutmeg. When roulade is cooked invert it on to a clean piece of greaseproof paper, peel away lining paper, and leave to cool slightly. Spread the sauce evenly over the surface, and roll up like a swiss roll. Sprinkle the top with grated cheese. Keep warm.

To freeze place in rigid plastic container.

To serve from frozen thaw out at room temperature for 2-3 hours, then place on baking sheet in preheated oven, Gas mark 4, 350°F, 175°C, for 20-30 mins.

Prep time: 20 mins
Cooking time: 15 mins plus 10 mins assembling　　　　*Catriona Godson*
Serves 6　　　　　　　　　　　　　　　　　　　*Chiddingfold*

ZAIRE CHICKEN

2 cups chopped onions	1 tblsp chopped fresh ginger
½ to 1½ tsp chopped chives	or ½ tsp ground
2 tblsp garlic	¼ tsp white pepper
1 tsp salt	1½ cups water
1 cup lemon juice	3½ lbs cut up chicken
3 tblsp sesame oil	or chicken joints

In glass dish combine onions, chopped garlic, chives, ginger, pepper and salt. Pour in lemon juice, 1 cup of water, 1 tblsp oil. Add chicken pieces and leave to marinate for 2-3 hours. Remove chicken pieces from marinade, saving juice and veg. Pat chicken pieces dry. Heat 2 tblsp oil, brown chicken pieces on all sides, remove and keep warm. Strain marinade, add veg from marinade to pan and cook 5 mins. Add chicken and juices from chicken, ½ cup of marinade and ¼ cup of water. Cook partially covered for 25 mins or till tender. Serve with fried rice.

Time: 45 mins plus marinating
Serves 5-6

Fried Rice

2 chopped onions	4 cups cold cooked rice
2 tsp soy sauce	1 tsp curry powder
s and p	2 tblsp sesame oil
2 tblsp butter	

In oil and butter cook two chopped onions till soft. Add cold cooked rice. When rice is warm, add soy sauce, curry powder and s and p to taste.

Time: 10 mins   *Bea Lacey*
Serves 5-6   *Yellow Springs, Ohio*

STUFFED CHICKEN BREASTS

4 boned chicken breasts (skin left on)	4 oz cooked chopped spinach
8 ox Philadelphia cheese	1 small egg
1 small onion	¼ tsp nutmeg
½ tsp savory	1 dessertsp chopped parsley
½ tsp oregano	freshly ground pepper
pinch of salt	1 oz butter

Chop the onion finely and cook in a little butter. Lightly beat egg. Mix together all of the other ingredients except for the butter, with onion and a little of the egg. Then lift up the skin from the breast by gently easing with a knife to begin with, running your finger between the flesh and the skin and taking care not to break the skin. Fill under the skin with the prepared mixture and fold the skin back over, tucking the ends underneath the chicken to seal in the stuffing. Place these in a shallow ovenproof dish which has been smeared with the butter. Season and cook in a preheated oven at Gas mark 4, 350°F, 175°C, for about ¾ hour until chicken is a golden brown. Baste from time to time. This recipe is marvellous both hot and cold. When having this cold, arrange the chicken in slices which enables you to show off the contrasting colour of the spinach and cheese stuffing cooked inside the chicken.

Prep time: 15 mins
Cooking time: 45 mins   *Sandra Macpherson of Glentruim*
Serves 4   *Newtonmore*

CHICKEN CACCIATORE

4 chicken pieces	2 cloves garlic, crushed
⅔ cups chopped onion	1½ cups green pepper, chopped
1½ tsp curry powder	⅔ tsp white pepper
1½ tsp thyme	2 tins tomatoes
1 tsp parsley	1 cup sliced toasted almonds
1 cup currants	butter, oil
1 tsp salt	1 cup sherry

Marinate chicken pieces in sherry and garlic for 2 hours. Season with s and p and roll in flour. Fry in a butter/oil mixture until brown and remove to a casserole. Sauter onion and peppers in some fat until soft. Add tomatoes, herbs, spices and sherry. Pour over chicken and bake at Gas mark 4, 360°F, 180°C, for 40 mins. Add currants and sprinkle almonds on top. Serve with saffron rice.

Time: 50 mins plus 2 hours marinating   *Penny Howman*
Serves 4   *Pitlochry*

CHICKEN WITH PEANUT BUTTER SAUCE

4 chicken quarters	2 tblsp flour
1 tsp dry mustard	s and p

Sauce:

2 tsp flour	3 tblsp peanut butter
½ pint chicken stock	2 tsp Worcester sauce
2 tsp lemon juice	1 tsp sugar
1 oz salted peanuts, chopped	

Coat the chicken with flour, with mustard, s and p added. Shallow fry in a covered pan for 30-40 mins until tender. Blend flour with peanut butter in a saucepan. Add the stock gradually, stirring all the time. Add Worcester sauce, lemon juice and sugar. Bring to the boil and simmer for 1 minute, stirring continuously. Add peanuts and serve the sauce poured over the chicken. Garnish with watercress.

Prep time: 15-20 mins
Cooking time: 40 mins approx
Serves 4

Margarite Campbell
Pitlochry

QUICK CHICKEN

1 oz butter or margarine
4 fl oz white wine
salt
pinch of paprika
approx 6 fl oz milk
6 oz sliced mushrooms

chicken joints (breasts or thighs)
2 level tblsp plain flour
freshly milled black pepper
¼ pint single cream
1 tblsp finely chopped onion

Fry chicken gently in butter or marg in saucepan for 20 mins, turn, add wine and cook for further 25 mins. Transfer to a dish or casserole and keep warm. To the juices add flour, salt and pepper, paprika, onion and mushrooms. Gradually add cream and milk and cook until thick. Pour over the chicken and serve with new potatoes and peas.

Prep time: 5 mins
Cooking time: 45 mins
Serves 4

Mary Horsfall
Kinloch Rannoch

CHICKEN SHERRY

3 chicken breasts, split
¼ cup sherry
¼ cup soy sauce
¼ cup salad oil

2 tblsp water
½ tsp ginger
1 tblsp brown sugar

Combine liquids and spice. Arrange chicken pieces in buttered baking dish. Pour wine mixture over chicken, cover and bake at Gas mark 4, 350°F, 175°C, for about 1½ hours. Good served with rice.

Prep time: 5 mins
Cooking time: 1½ hours
Serves 2-3

Elsie Macnaughton
Pitlochry

WOK CHICKEN AND VEGETABLES STIR FRIED WITH WALNUTS

left over cooked chicken or turkey
¼ lb sliced mushrooms
water chestnuts
bean shoots
¼ lb chopped walnuts
2 tblsp sherry
1 tblsp flour
1 large onion, chopped
s and p

bean sprouts
2 sticks celery, sliced
1 carrot, thinly sliced
soy sauce
½ cup chicken stock
1 clove garlic, crushed
oil
chopped parsley

Stir fry onions, garlic, carrots and celery in oil in wok. Add the bean shoots, water chestnuts and bean sprouts. Then add mushrooms and chicken. Stir fry for a few minutes. Add about 1 tblsp soy sauce, mix in the flour and stir fry for about 30 secs. Add the chicken stock and the sherry. Allow to thicken. Add the walnuts and stir fry for 1 minute. Season, add some chopped parsley and serve with rice.

Prep time: 10 mins
Cooking time: 10 mins   *Jenny Abramsky*
Serves 6   *London*

CHICKEN IN CURRY MAYONNAISE

1 cooked chicken

Curry mayonnaise:
  1 tblsp oil
  1 level tblsp curry powder
  ¼ pint stock
  juice of ½ lemon
  ½ pint mayonnaise

1 small onion
¼ pint stock
1 rounded tsp tomato purée
2 rounded tblsp sweet chutney
3 tblsp single cream

Heat oil in saucepan. Peel and finely chop onion, add to pan, cover and fry until soft. Stir in curry powder and cook a further few mins. Stir in stock, tomato purée, lemon juice and chutney. Stir until boiling, then simmer for 5 mins. Draw off heat and strain into a basin. Allow to cool, stir in the mayonnaise and cream. Remove flesh from chicken in chunky pieces and arrange in a serving dish. Spoon over the curry mayonnaise and serve with a rice salad which includes chopped green pepper, chunks of pineapple, flaked almonds and a few seedless raisins, all tossed in a dressing of oil and vinegar. A nice supper dish for guests.

Time: 20 mins   *Roberta Mackie*
Serves 6   *Dundee*

CHICKEN OR HAM MOUSSE

3 cups minced chicken
½ cup salad dressing
(mayonnaise is better)
½ cup cold chicken stock
garlic

2 tblsp lemon juice
¾ tsp ground celery seed
s and p
¾ cup heavy whipped cream
2 tsp gelatine

Blend chicken, salad dressing or mayonnaise, lemon juice, celery seed. Fold in the whipped cream, season to taste. Melt gelatine in a cup over hot water, add to chicken stock and fold into chicken mixture. Pour into a mould to set.

Ham can be used instead of chicken and chopped mushrooms are a good addition to this dish.

There is no need to use cream as a small tin of condensed milk from the fridge will whip satisfactorily and can be used instead. If using crab meat instead of chicken, mix brown and white meat together. A small onion, chopped and softened in butter can be added and the garlic, which is optional, should be treated in the same way. Tomatoes, tomato paste and chopped parsley can vary the recipe.

Prep time: 20 mins
No cooking
Serves 6

Ruth Hope
Somerford Keynes

PHEASANT CARRICKMHOR

2 pheasant breasts
2 onions cut into rings
2 oz sultanas

1 pint red wine
1 oz butter
½ pint double cream

On to foil lay onion rings, sultanas and pheasant breasts. Pour wine over, season, put butter on each breast and wrap into airtight parcel with foil. Cook at Gas mark 8, 450°F, 230°C, for 30-35 mins then at Gas mark 4, 340°F, 170°C, for 1-1½ hours. Remove breasts, pour other ingredients into pan. Reduce liquid to ¼ pint. Season, stir in cream and boil for a few mins to thicken. Slice breasts and lay in dish. Pour sauce over meat and serve.

Prep time: 10 mins
Cooking time: 2½ hours
Serves 2-4 depending on size of bird

Di Barbour
Dunkeld

PHEASANT WITH WHISKY

2 oz butter   1-2 pheasants, depending on size (cleaned)
1 onion, finely chopped   ½ cup whisky
⅔ cup beef stock   s and p
Pinch paprika   5 juniper berries
½ cup double cream   1 tsp lemon juice

Melt butter in a flame proof casserole, add pheasant and brown on all sides, remove from pan with a slotted spoon. Add onion to the pan and cook until soft and golden brown. Warm half the whisky by standing it in a jug of hot water for a few seconds, return the pheasant to the pan, pour the whisky over and carefully ignite. Pour on the stock and add the salt, pepper, paprika and the juniper berries, bring to the boil. Place in a preheated oven, Gas mark 4, 350°F, 180°C, and cook for 1 hour until tender. When the pheasant is tender, remove from the pan and joint it – cut off the legs and divide into two, remove breast and cut in two. Discard the wings, arrange pheasant on a heated serving dish. Boil the sauce until syrupy, add the remaining whisky, cream and lemon juice, taste and adjust the seasoning. Reheat without the sauce coming to the boil. Strain the sauce over the pheasant, serve with green beans.

Prep time: 15-20 mins
Cooking time: 1½ hours   *Douglas Battison*
Serves 3-4   *Pitlochry*

PHEASANT AUX CHOUX

1 pheasant   1 med hard white cabbage
1 large onion   ½ lb sausage meat made into balls
1 smoked pork sausage   and rolled in flour
   (U shaped)   ½ lb bacon

Sauce:
   flour   2 lumps sugar
   stock   nutmeg
   s and p   grated lemon peel
   juniper berries   port or red wine
   2 clove garlic

Cook pheasant for ¾ hour in butter in a heavy pan, covered, on top of stove, turning over once or twice, so that each side is nicely browned. Carve it off the bone and make stock of the carcass. Slice cabbage and blanch in boiling water for 5 mins. Fry onion and then make a sauce with flour and stock, season with salt, pepper, a few juniper berries (crushed), 2 cloves garlic, 2 lumps sugar, nutmeg and a little grated lemon peel and port or red wine. Assemble all ingredients by first putting some sauce in bottom of large casserole then layers of alternate cabbage, pheasant, sausage balls and sliced smoked sausage and sauce, ending up with a layer of cabbage. Cover entire top with sliced bacon and cook in moderate oven, Gas mark 4, 350°F, 180°C. You will be amazed how many this one pheasant will feed.

Prep time: 45 mins
Cooking time: 1 hour
Serves 6-7

Ann Dixon
London

PHEASANT IN HOT DEVILLED SAUCE

This can be made just as well with cooked chicken.

1 tblsp Worcester sauce	cooked pheasant
½ pint single cream	curry powder
1 tblsp made mustard	chutney

Cut into neat slices, portions of cooked pheasant. Lay in deep pyrex dish. Beat sauce ingredients together and pour over bird. Bake slowly till light brown, Gas mark 3, 340°F, 170°C. Serve with cooked rice, flavoured with curry powder to taste and 1 large tblsp chutney.

Prep time: 10 mins
Cooking time: 10-15 mins
Serves 4-6

Rosalind Stewart-Wilson
Pitlochry

PHEASANT GOUGERE

A useful way of using up left over game etc. An easy but impressive looking dish.

Choux pastry:

4 oz plain flour	4 oz butter or hard margarine
good pinch of salt	¼ pint milk
¼ pint water	4 beaten eggs

Melt fat in liquids and bring to boil. Pour flour and salt in, all at once and beat hard. Add eggs a bit at a time, beating until shiny, and paste leaves sides of pan.

Filling:

1 lb chopped cooked game	½ pint stock
1 large onion, chopped	½ tsp thyme
1 x 16 oz can tomatoes, chopped	1 apple, grated
½ tsp mustard powder	1 carrot, grated
2 oz margarine	s and p
2 tblsp plain flour	

Fry the onion in margarine until just golden. Add flour and mix well. Add mustard powder, gradually add stock and tomatoes. Cook slowly until thick, stirring constantly. Add apple, carrot and meat, season. Grease a fairly shallow ovenproof dish. Spread pastry all round edge, roughly (which looks more attractive). Pile filling in centre, and cover loosely with foil so that it doesn't dry up. Do not cover choux pastry. Bake in oven, Gas mark 5, 370°F, 185°C, for 40-45 mins, until pastry is well risen and golden brown. Serve immediately with salad or green vegetables.

Prep time: 30 mins
Cooking time: 40-45 mins
Serves 6-8

Susan Dixon
London

BLACKCOCK STEW

(This recipe may also be used with old grouse or pigeons.)

2 blackcock or grey hens	½ lb cubed bacon
8 onions	8 carrots
½ head of celery	½ lb mushrooms
2 cloves garlic	2 tblsp tomato purée
1 dessrtsp molasses sugar	1 tin beer
1 small tin pimentoes	2 tsp arrowroot
2 tblsp port	s and p
dried oregano or fresh thyme	3 tblsp croutons
2 tblsp oil and Flora marg	chopped parsley

Brown birds in oil and Flora over medium heat in a frying pan with bacon. Meanwhile cut up vegetables not too finely. Put birds in pressure cooker and fry up vegetables but do not brown. While they are cooking, add crushed garlic, plenty oregano or thyme and heaped dessrtsp of molasses sugar, tomato purée, s and p. Put vegetables in pressure cooker with birds (which should be cut in half if necessary). Add tin of beer, bring to pressure and cook for 20 mins. Remove birds, discard bones and arrange meat neatly in serving dish. Slake arrowroot in port wine and add to vegetables and gravy in pressure cooker. Bring to the boil and simmer until slightly thickened. Pour over meat and decorate top with half a small tin of pimentoes, finely sliced. Adjust seasoning and keep warm in oven until ready to serve, topped with croutons and chopped parsley.

NB: The remaining half tin of pimentoes may be used for making a piperade. If there is any blackcock stew left over, it may be liquidised with a little extra stock and sprinkled with chopped parsley to make an excellent soup.

Prep time: 20 mins
Cooking time: 30 mins, if pressure cooked
or 2-3 hours in low oven or
just simmer for 2-3 hours on top of stove

Elizabeth Lyle
Dunkeld

RABBIT, HARE OR CHICKEN CASSEROLE

1 hare, rabbit or chicken	1 lb chopped carrots
1 pint chicken or ham stock	1 lb potatoes, sliced
3 large onions, sliced	4 cooking apples
1 bay leaf	pinch of thyme
½ tsp parsley	½ oz flour
s and p	4 rashers bacon, chopped
1 tsp sugar	fat for frying

Cut meat into small pieces. Melt fat in pan, brown meat and bacon and place in casserole dish. Add vegetables, seasoning, stock and flour (made into a sauce with some stock). Add apples, chopped, and sugar, cover dish and place in oven, at Gas mark 5, 375°F, 190°C, for 2 hours. Check for liquid after half cooking time and add more if necessary.

Prep time: 15 mins
Cooking time: 2 hours   *Peter Barr*
Serves 5   *Banbury*

JUGGED PIGEON

2 or 3 pigeons	1 oz dripping
2 onions, sliced	bouquet garni
6 cloves	3 whole allspice
½ tsp pepper	salt
1 tsp grated lemon rind	1 oz butter or marg
4 tblsp flour	¼ pint vinegar
½ pint red wine, cider or beer	

Joint the pigeons and fry the pieces until brown in the dripping. Put in a casserole with the onion and seasonings. Melt the butter or marg and add the flour. Mix well and stir in the liquid. Stir until it boils and pour over the pigeons. Cover and cook in a slow oven for 3-4 hours, at Gas mark 4, 370°F, 185°C. This recipe can also be used for hare, rabbit or venison, using 1 hare or 2 small rabbits or 2 lbs venison.

Prep time: 30 mins
Cooking time: 3-4 hours   *Mollie Sugden*
Serves 6   *Surrey*

CERVO CON SALSA DI CILIEGIE
(VENISON WITH CHERRY SAUCE)

3 lbs venison

For marinade:

1 sliced onion	2 cloves garlic
1 chopped carrot	2 bay leaves
1 sliced stick celery	thyme or marjoram
1 cup olive oil	s and p
1 tblsp crushed coriander seeds	½ bottle red wine

To cook with meat:

1 sliced onion	a few mushrooms
1 sliced carrot	mixed herbs (no sage or rosemary)
2 teacups water	1 clove garlic
s and p	thick slice ham or bacon
fat for frying	

For cherry sauce:

big cup bottled stored cherries	black pepper
2 tblsp redcurrant jelly	1 tsp wine vinegar
1 dessertsp crushed coriander	

Marinade:

Heat olive oil and lightly brown onion, carrot and celery. Cook 5 mins. Add garlic, bay leaves, thyme or marjoram, s and p and coriander seeds. Pour in wine and simmer for about 15 mins. Cool. Pour over meat, leave venison to marinade for 2 days, turning a few times.

To cook meat:

Remove meat from marinade and free it from any vegetables. Brown in hot fat, put it in an earthenware vessel if possible, but a roasting tin or casserole dish will do. It should fit snugly without any space to spare. In the same fat fry the carrot and onion. Strain the marinade and bring it to the boil. Add water, mushrooms, herbs, garlic and s and p. Boil again and pour over meat. Lay ham or bacon over top, cover with foil and tight lid and cook in a slow oven, Gas mark 1, 300°F, 150°C, for 3½ hours.

Cherry sauce: Dissolve jelly in pan. Add cherries and a little of their juice. Add a pinch of black pepper, vinegar and coriander seeds and simmer 5 mins. 15 mins before serving, press all liquid and veg from venison, through a sieve. Keep meat hot in the covered pot, reduce liquid and veg mix to ⅔ of its volume by rapidly boiling. Add to cherry sauce and pour over meat. Cut bacon (or ham) into squares and put round meat – reheat for a few mins.

Prep time: marinade 25 mins (leave for 2 days)   *Hazel Barbour*
Cooking time: 3½ hours (+ 15 mins making sauce)   *Fincastle*

DEEP FROZEN MEAT

3 lbs frozen elk or beefsteak, boned or venison.

Brine:

1 pint water	¾ cup salt
1 tiny spoonful salt petre	

In the lowest oven you can manage, put the frozen meat in a dish, and cook for 12 hours. Mix the brine and put the steak in a plastic bag, with the brine for 4-5 hours. Serve cold in slices with potato gratin and a fresh salad.

(Oven at 95°F)   *Ingrid Wikstrom*
                                                                         Sweden

GROUSE A LA CREME

3 young grouse, halved
6 slices toast
24 chopped mushrooms
¾ pint cream

6 oz butter
6 slices cold boiled gammon
s and p

Put one ounce of butter under each piece of toast, in a large casserole. Lay a slice of gammon on top of toast, and top each one with half a raw grouse. Season, and add chopped mushrooms. Pour over the cream. Cover the dish, and cook slowly on top of stove, on an asbestos mat, for 35 mins. (An old bird will take longer.) Baste often with a little more cream as the sauce reduces. The butter and juices from birds, and the cream, amalgamate into a rich and tasty sauce. Serve immediately with plain boiled potatoes.

Prep time: 5 mins
Cooking time: 35 mins
Serves 0

Barbara Liddell
Pitlochry

SALMI OF GAME

1 lightly roasted pheasant
  (or similar game bird)
12 button mushrooms
small pieces cooked puff pastry

4 tblsp port
6 glacé cherries
1 tblsp redcurrant jelly
s and p

Remove skin from bird, and divide into portions. Put in a heavy flame-proof casserole. Cover with the sauce, port, jelly and mushroom stalks. Simmer slowly under tender (1-1½ hrs). Arrange meat on a hot dish. Strain the sauce and skim off any fat. Pour sauce over meat, and garnish with sautéd mushrooms, cherries (halved) and pastry pieces.

Prep time: 5 mins
Cooking time: 1-1½ hrs
Serves 4

Barbara Liddell
Pitlochry

To "love and honour" are OK
And one might promise to obey
But what makes wives turn slowly grey
Is what to cook each blessed day!

American

Chapter 4

SALADS –
VEGETARIAN – VEGETABLES

BEA'S POTATO SALAD

2¼ lbs potatoes (ones that boil soft)
1 soup sp bovril and 1 stock cube,
  chicken or beef, dissolved in
  3½ fl oz boiling water

7 fl oz dry white wine
5 chopped shallots

Mustard sauce:
4 soup sp wine vinegar
mustard
½ soup sp salt

oil
1 coffee sp s and p

Steam potatoes for 30 or 40 mins, better to overcook than under. Add white wine to potatoes when cooked and still hot, at room temperature. Make mustard sauce with mustard, oil and other ingredients and mix over potatoes while still hot. Serve tepid.

Prep time: 5 mins
Cooking time: 40 mins
Serves 4-6

Bea Lacey
Yellow Springs, USA

POTATO SALAD

1 lb cooked potatoes
1 tblsp chopped parsley
1 cup salad cream
1 tblsp vinegar

3 tblsp chopped chives
s and p
1 tblsp cream
1 tsp sugar

Chop potatoes into cubes. Add chives. Mix together any bought salad cream with the cream, vinegar and sugar. Add seasoning and pour over potatoes. Toss and turn into serving dish. Sprinkle with chopped parsley.

Time: 10 mins
Serves 4-6

Iris Colin
Louth

POTATO SALAD WITH LEMON DRESSING

6 med sized potatoes
¼ pint hot chicken stock
1 tblsp vinegar
1 tsp finely grated lemon rind
3 tblsp thinly sliced spring onion
¼ tsp freshly ground black pepper
chopped parsley

6 tblsp fresh lemon juice
5 tblsp oil
1 tsp sugar
1 tsp capers
1 tsp salt
2 tblsp finely diced celery

Boil potatoes in their jackets. Peel off the skins and slice thinly into a bowl whilst hot. Blend lemon juice, vinegar, oil, chicken stock, sugar, lemon rind, spring onions and capers together in a bowl, add s and p and celery and whisk for about 1 min. Pour over the potato slices. Allow to cool but do not chill. Sprinkle on chopped parsley.

To make a supper dish, add to the above 4 tblsp thin slices of ham, chopped hard boiled egg and 4 tblsp cream.

Prep time: 20 mins
Cooking time: 30 mins
Serves 4-6 as supper dish
     6-8 as salad

Vivien Rossaak
Johannesburg

CUCUMBER AND YOGHOURT SALAD

2 large cucumbers
parsley and mint

2 tubs yoghourt
s and p

Cube unpeeled cucumbers and put in a bowl, pour over the yoghourt and sprinkle with s and p. Toss. Turn into serving dish and sprinkle with a mixture of chopped parsley and mint. Refrigerate for 3 hours.

Time: 10 mins plus 3 hours in fridge
Serves 4-6

Iris Colin
Louth

CREAM CHEESE AND CUCUMBER RING

12 oz cucumber unpeeled
6 level tsp gelatine
1¼ lb full fat soft cream cheese
4 tblsp milk
¼ level tsp paprika
freshly milled pepper

6 tblsp water
3 tblsp lemon juice
7 fl oz thick mayonnaise
¼ level tsp salt
2 egg whites

Slice some cucumber thinly and arrange overlapping in base of a 3 pint capacity plain ring mould. Dice the remainder. Dissolve the gelatine in lemon juice and water. Cool a little. Place cheese, milk, mayonnaise and seasonings in a deep bowl and whisk until evenly blended. Fold a little cream cheese mixture into gelatine and then add this to the rest of the cheese mixture. Stir in diced cucumber. Whisk egg whites until stiff. Using metal spoon fold into cheese mixture until evenly blended. Turn into mould and chill until set. This goes well with salads, or as part of a cold buffet.

Prep time: 20-30 mins
No cooking   *Catriona Godson*
Serves 6   *Chiddingfold*

CUCUMBER CHARTREUSE

1 lime jelly tablet   ¼ pint cider vinegar
2 level tsp sugar   drop of green colouring
8 oz cucumber, diced and skinned

Place jelly cubes in 1 pint measure and make up to ¾ pint with hot water. Stir until jelly has melted. Add vinegar, sugar and a drop of colouring, leave to cool until consistency of egg white. Fold in cucumber and when this is evenly suspended pour mixture into a 1½ pint mould. Leave to set and then unmould. The sharpness of this chartreuse gives a good balance to a rich fish dish such as salmon, and is delicious with it.

Time: 10 mins   *Marigold Hay*
Serves 6   *Comrie*

SWEETCORN AND PRAWN SALAD

1 head of chicory   12 oz can sweetcorn
8 oz prawns or cooked chicken   4 oz Cheshire cheese
1 recipe banana dressing (see below)   pimento

Separate leaves of chicory, wash well and drain. Arrange on round platter, radiating from centre. Drain sweet corn. Tip into bowl. Cut chicken (if used) into bite-size pieces. Cut cheese into small cubes, add to corn and mix well. If not chicken, add prawns. Pour dressing over corn mixture and toss. Pile on to the centre of dish over chicory leaves. Garnish with trails of pimento strips.

Dressing:
2 med sized bananas   2 tblsp lemon juice
5 tblsp mayonnaise   5 oz carton natural yoghourt
1 level tsp bottled horseradish sauce   ½ level tsp icing or castor sugar
½ level tsp salt   pinch cayenne pepper

Mash bananas finely, beat in lemon juice, mayonnaise, yoghourt, horseradish sauce and sugar. Season to taste with salt and pepper. Use immediately.

Prep time: 30 mins   *Christine Kinnear*
No cooking   *BBC Radio Scotland*

BULGAR

Bulgar is made up of wholewheat grains which have been soaked well and then toasted to a very high temperture until they crack. As a result it needs little or no cooking.

BULGAR GRAPE SALAD

6 oz bulgar (obtainable from
   health food shops)
1 oz currants
1½ oz whole almonds, toasted

2 sticks celery sliced
3 oz black grapes
   halved and pipped

Dressing:
3 tblsp sunflower oil
1 tblsp white wine vinegar
s and p

¼ level tsp mustard powder
grated rind and juice of ½ a lemon
1 tblsp Tahini paste (health food
   shops or delicatessan)

Soak bulgar in a bowl in cold water, to cover by about 1 centimetre, for 30 mins. Drain and dry in sieve over empty bowl for about 30 mins. Mix dressing, add all other ingredients and dressing, and serve as a salad with cold meats, quiches, etc.

Time: 1 hour
Serves 6

Barbara Liddell
Pitlochry

TABOULI BULGAR SALAD

7 ozs bulgar
2 med tomatoes, peeled, deseeded
   and finely chopped
½ cup fresh parsley, finely chopped
½ cup fresh coriander, finely chopped
   (if fresh coriander not available
   use 1 tsp ground coriander)

1 med onion, finely chopped
   or 4 spring onions, incl
   2" green tops also finely
   chopped
½ cup fresh mint finely
   chopped
⅓ cup lemon juice

Soak bulgar in cold water for 30 mins, covering bulgar by about 1 cm of the water. Drain in wire sieve over empty bowl for 30 mins. Mix all ingredients in a bowl, forking over lightly. The herbs are measured after chopping.

Time: 1 hour
Serves 8 as a salad
less if vegetarian

Barbara Liddell
Pitlochry

BEETROOT AND ORANGE SALAD

1 med beetroot per person	2 oranges
1 onion	olive oil
s and p	

Slice up cooked, peeled beetroots, or coarsely grate raw ones. Mix with thinly sliced oranges and onion and 2 tblsp olive oil, s and p. Grated zest of orange is also good with beetroot.

Time: 10 mins   *Sonia Yellowlees*
Serves 6   *Aberfeldy*

COLESLAW WHICH KEEPS

Chop in processor:

2 large or 3 med cabbages	1 onion
2 stalks celery	3 or 4 carrots

Sprinkle generously with salt and set aside whilst making dressing. Before adding the dressing, put vegetables in a tea towel and squeeze dry.

Dressing:
Combine in a saucepan –

2 cups sugar	1 cup vinegar
1 tsp salt	$1/8$ tsp pepper
1 or 2 tsp celery seed	

Bring to boil, remove from heat. When cool add to cabbage mixture and mix well.

Prep time: 10 mins
No cooking   *Ann Maxwell*
Serves 8   *Pitlochry*

MIXED BEAN SALAD

1 tin green beans	1 tin barlotti beans	lemon juice
1 tin broad beans	corn oil	sugar
1 tin chick beans	vinegar	
1 tin kidney beans	white wine	

Drain beans from tins, mix all together, marinade in the following overnight: equal quantities of corn oil and vinegar and white wine (to make up to ½ pint);
1 dessertsp lemon juice; sugar to taste (at least 1 tblsp). Drain and put in bowl. Note: ideal in these quantities for parties.

Prep time: 15-20 mins   *Norman Jamieson*
                                                              Perth

ICED PEAR AND CHEESE SALAD

3 tblsp mayonnaise
1 canned red pepper
2 large pears
watercress sprigs to garnish

4 oz crumbled Cheshire cheese
1/8 pint double cream
4 lettuce leaves

Mix mayonnaise, cream, cheese and chopped pepper. Spread in a shallow dish. Freeze for approx 1½ hours, stirring every ½ hour or so. Wipe and peel pears. Cut in half and remove core. Place each pear-half on a lettuce leaf, pile iced cheese mixture on pears, garnish with watercress and serve immediately.

Prep time: 5 mins
No cooking
Freezing: 1½ hours
Serves 4

Sheila Turner
Pitlochry

CABBAGE, CHEESE AND RAISIN SALAD

8 oz shredded raw cabbage
2 oz raisins
½ level tsp salt

8 oz grated cheddar cheese
4 tblsp mayonnaise
pinch cayenne pepper

Toss all the ingredients lightly together and serve with cold meats.

Time: 10 mins
Serves 4-6

Sheila Turner
Pitlochry

MARINATED MUSHROOM SALAD

2 lb button mushrooms
4 tblsp chopped parsley
4 tblsp chopped chives
½ tsp salt

½ pint salad oil
¼ pint lemon juice
¼ tsp black pepper
¼ pint vinegar

Slice mushrooms thinly. Layer in dish with parsley and chives. Whisk all other ingredients together until thick and creamy, and pour over dish.

Prep time: 15 mins
No Cooking
Serves 8

Barbara Liddell
Pitlochry

SPINACH AND LEMON SALAD

Cook spinach as usual and drain and chop. Serve hot or cold, with olive oil, s and p, and lemon juice, never vinegar.

Barbara Liddell
Pitlochry

RAW SPINACH AND BACON SALAD

1 lb of youngest spinach leaves   light malt vinegar
garlic   s and p
6 slices streaky bacon

Rub a bowl with cut side of a clove of garlic. Put spinach leaves in bowl and season with s and p. Sauter six scissor-snipped slices bacon until bacon fat has melted. Pour it boiling hot over spinach, and immediately sprinkle with malt vinegar. Toss quickly and thoroughly and serve at once.

Prep and cooking time: 10 mins   *Barbara Liddell*
Serves 2   *Pitlochry*

GARLIC SPINACH

.1 lb spinach   4 tblsp olive oil
2 cloves garlic

Cook spinach in its own water and drain well. Sauter 2 cloves garlic in 4 tblsp olive oil until golden. Strain off oil, and pour over spinach, discarding garlic. Toss spinach well until it shines. Season with s and p.

Prep time: 10-15 mins
Cooking time: 00 mins   *Barbara Liddell*
Serves 2   *Pitlochry*

PUREE OF FRENCH BEANS

1 ¼ lbs French beans
1 soup sp fresh cream
1 soup sp melted butter

2 ½ pint water
1 oz sea salt
s and p

Boil beans for 10 mins in water with sea salt. Then drain and put in ice cold water. (This prevents further cooking and removes surplus salt, which preserves colour whilst cooking.) Drain again and purée in mixer or liquidiser. Add fresh cream and melted butter. Keep hot in a bowl over hot water before serving. Add s and p to taste. The purée can be frozen, before adding cream and butter.

Prep time: 10-15 mins
Cooking time: 10 mins
Serves 4-6

Rose Uren
London

HARICOT AND ONION CASSEROLE

8 oz haricot beans
freshly ground black pepper
¾ pint water
2 oz marg
2 oz grated cheese
8 oz tinned tomatoes, chopped

sea salt
1 lb onions
approx ½ pint milk
2 oz flour
½ tsp dry mustard

Soak, drain and rinse the beans, cover them with water and let them simmer gently for about an hour, or until tender. Drain, season with sea salt and pepper. Preheat the oven to Gas mark 5, 375°F, 190°C. Peel and slice the onions and cook them gently in the water until they are tender, then drain them reserving the water and making it up to 1 pint with the milk, keeping onions. Melt marg in a saucepan and add the flour, when it froths remove the saucepan from the heat and add the milk and onion water. Return the saucepan to the heat, stirring all the time for 3 mins, until the sauce has thickened. Add the grated cheese and the dry mustard, salt and pepper. Put the beans into a shallow greased casserole dish and arrange the tomatoes on top, season with s and p. Put the onions on top of the tomatoes and season again, finally pour the sauce evenly over the onions. Scatter a few dried breadcrumbs over the top, dot with marg and bake for 30-40 mins. Serve with potatoes and a green vegetable.

Prep time: 10 mins
Cooking time: 1 hour
Serves 4

Joby Jackson
Pitlochry

ARTICHOKE SOUFFLE

bechamel sauce made with ½ pint milk
1 oz flour
4 oz puréed Jerusalem artichokes
   (about 1½ lb)

1 oz butter
4 eggs
3 cloves garlic
1 tsp coriander seeds

Make a bechamel sauce, cool and add the egg yolks. In another pan fry the chopped garlic very gently in some butter, crush the coriander seeds with the flat of a knife and add them and the artichoke purée to the garlic. When this mixture is warm, add to the bechamel sauce with s and p to taste. Whip whites till stiff and fold into the above mixture. Turn into a buttered souffle dish and bake in oven, Gas mark 5, 375°F, 190°C, for 20-25 mins. Serve with a crisp green salad.

Prep time: 30 mins (if artichokes not too knobbly)
Cooking time: 25 mins
Serves 4

Henrietta Thewes
Killiecrankie

SPINACH SOUFFLE WITH ANCHOVY SAUCE

2 oz butter
2 oz flour
s and p
nutmeg
¾ pint milk

6 eggs
cooked spinach, drained and chopped finely
4 anchovies
cream
lemon juice

Sauce:

½ pint bechamel sauce, mixed with 4 finely chopped anchovies, cream and lemon juice to taste.

Melt butter, stir in flour. Season. Add milk and cook until sauce thickens, stirring all the time. Remove from heat, quickly stir in egg yolks. Add spinach. Beat egg whites till very stiff and fold into mixture. Turn into buttered soufflé dish, cook at Gas mark 3, 325°F, 165°C, for 40 mins. Serve with anchovy sauce. You can prepare this up to 4 hours in advance and refrigerate it, and then add 10 mins to cooking time. Feel free to open the oven door and look at it!

Prep time: 15 mins
Cooking time: 40 mins
Serves 4-6

Lavinia Gordon
Blair Atholl

SPINACH AND LENTIL ROULADE

6 oz red lentils
1 small onion, skinned and
finely chopped
2 level tblsp tomato ketchup
1 level tblsp creamed horseradish
4 oz butter
salt and freshly ground pepper

1 lb spinach, cleaned and trimmed
(frozen spinach can be substituted)
2 oz wholemeal flour
2 eggs separated
½ pint milk
dry breadcrumbs

Butter and line 11" swiss roll tin. Cook lentils with onion in a large saucepan of boiling salted water until tender, drain well. Return to pan and heat to evaporate excess moisture, add tomato ketchup, horseradish and 2 oz butter. Rub through a sieve, or purée in a blender, season and set aside. In a pan gently cook spinach, sprinkled with salt (do not add any liquid) for 3-4 mins. Turn into a colander, press with a potato masher and chop finely. To make the sauce, melt remaining butter in a pan, stirring in the flour and cook gently for 1 min. Remove from the heat and gradually stir in milk, bring to boil and continue to cook, stirring until the sauce thickens. Remove from the heat, stir in spinach and egg yolks. Season. Whisk egg whites until stiff, gently fold into spinach mixture, spoon into prepared tin. Level surface. Bake in oven at Gas mark 6, 400°F, 205°C, for 20 mins until well risen and golden, turn out on to greaseproof paper sprinkled with dried breadcrumbs, peel off greaseproof lining. Spread lentil purée over surface. Roll up swiss roll style and return to oven for 5 mins.

Prep time: 20 mins
Cooking time: 50 mins
Serves 4-6

Sunny Ormonde
Chester

HUNGARIAN SPINACH

1 box frozen chopped spinach
1 tblsp flour
1 egg yolk
1 clove garlic

1 oz cooking oil, or chicken dripping
1 bouillon cube or 1 cupful hot stock
ground pepper

Defrost spinach and cook in 1 cupful of water. Make a roux with the fat and flour. Add the very finely chopped garlic clove, and the spinach purée. Dilute with hot stock, or bouillon cube dissolved in 1 cupful of water. Flavour with freshly ground pepper and bring to boil. Just prior to serving add one well beaten egg yolk, and beat into the hot spinach. The consistency should be creamy.

Prep time: defrosting frozen spinach
Cooking time: 10-15 mins
Serves 4

Eci Mackay
Pitlochry

VEGETARIAN MOUSSAKA

Dish:

1 lb kidney beans	2 tins plum tomatoes
1 lb onions	½ lb mushrooms
2 green peppers	½ lb aubergines (optional)
1 lb courgettes	mixed herbs
2 cloves garlic, crushed	s and p

Sauce:

2 egg yolks	¼ pint single cream
6 oz grated cheese	

Leave kidney beans to soak overnight. Boil in fresh water till soft. Meanwhile slice all vegetables. Fry in following order in oil or butter in a large deep pan: onions and pepper till almost cooked, then mushrooms, courgettes and crushed garlic. Finally add tomatoes and seasoning. Put all into a casserole with the kidney beans. The vegetables may either be cooked early and left to heat up, or alternatively kept hot in the oven. The sauce must be poured over the vegetables in their last 5 mins of heating. Beat egg yolks into cream, add grated cheese and seasoning. Melt in a saucepan and pour over vegetables. Serve with fresh green salad and hot garlic bread.

Prep time: start night before, 30 mins
Cooking time: 10 mins
Serves 6

Clare Musson
Glenalmond

POTATOES IN PAPRIKA SAUCE
(KRUMPCI PAPRIKAS)

1 ½ lb potatoes	1 tsp salt
3 oz lard, or bacon dripping	1 tsp paprika
1 large onion	1 green pepper
1 rasher bacon	1 fresh tomato

Peel potatoes and cut them in four. Heat lard, add finely chopped onion and fry till golden. Remove from heat and add paprika and sliced green pepper, tomato, potatoes, salt and slice of bacon. Add just enough water to cover. Bring to boil, and then reduce heat. Cook covered on low heat until the potatoes are ready. Serve in a deep dish, sprinkle the top with a spoonful of sour cream before serving. Serve with a crisp green salad.

Prep time: 15 mins
Cooking time: 20 mins
Serves 4

Eci Mackay
Pitlochry

BARBINO

3 tblsp good olive oil	2 small or 1 large bulb fennel
2 small or 1 large aubergine	1 can chick peas
1 can tomatoes	2 cloves garlic
s and p	red wine to taste

Cut aubergines into chunks, sprinkle with salt and leave for 20 mins to draw out bitter juices. Quarter fennel and rinse if necessary. Chop garlic finely. Fry garlic and fennel in oil till slightly brown, remove from pan, add rinsed and patted dry aubergines and slightly brown them. Return fennel and garlic to pan, with chick peas and tomatoes. Season to taste and add slurp of red wine. Cover and cook over low heat for 20 mins, or until fennel is tender.

Prep time: 25 mins
Cooking time: 20 mins
Serves 2 as main course   *Henrietta Thewes*
       4 as a veg or starter   *Killiecrankie*

RICE CASSEROLE

2 cups cooked rice	1 cup chopped parsley
1 cup grated cheese	2 cups milk
1/3 cup oil	1 grated onion
1 crushed clove garlic	1 tsp salt
2 beaten eggs	½ cup sautéed mushrooms

Mix cheese with rice and all other ingredients and bake in a greased casserole for 45 mins at Gas mark 4, 350°F, 175°C.

Prep time: 15 mins
Cooking time: 45 mins   *Elsie Macnaughton*
Serves 6-8   *Pitlochry*

RATATOUILLE FLAN – OR RATTY PIE

4 oz short crust pastry   2 oz grated cheese

For filling:

2 tblsp oil	1 clove garlic
1 med onion	1 lb courgetes or marrow
1 green pepper	4 tomatoes
1 level tsp sugar	s and p
3 eggs	

Roll out pastry and line an 8" quiche tin or buttered flan dish. Heat oil, add peeled and sliced onion, finely shredded and deseeded green pepper, and fry for a few mins to soften. Then add crushed garlic, and peeled and sliced courgettes. Peel tomatoes, deseed and add chopped flesh with sugar, s and p. Cover and cook gently for about 30 mins. Drain off and cool a few mins, then stir in beaten eggs and check seasoning. Pour into pastry case. Sprinkle with grated cheese, set above centre in mod hot oven at Gas mark 5, 375°F, 190°C and bake for 40 mins. Serve hot or cold.

Prep time: 30 mins
Cooking time: 30+40 mins   *Diana Macnab of Macnab*
Serves 4   *Killin*

STUFFED COURGETTES

8 courgettes (the smaller ones are not so bitter)	2 oz butter
4 oz mushrooms (optional)	1 med onion
4 oz brown breadcrumbs	3 oz cheddar cheese, grated
1 tsp mixed fresh herbs (or pinch of dried)	1 clove garlic, crushed (optional)

Wash the courgettes, top and tail and cut in half lengthways, simmer in salted water for five or ten mins. Courgettes should still be quite firm. Drain well. Scoop out pulp from centres with teaspoon, or a serrated grapefruit spoon is ideal, and mash a little. Meanwhile fry mushrooms, onions and garlic in butter until soft (about 6 mins), add pulp, crumbs, cheese and herbs. Stir and season well. Pack mixture into shells and sprinkle with some of the cheese and crumbs which you have kept on one side. Brown under grill. If you need to reheat, bake in oven in well buttered dish for 25 mins at Gas mark 5, 375°F, 190°C. This can be served as a starter or as a main course with brown rice and home-made tomato sauce, or as a special vegetable with the roast and potatoes. Make them in advance, sprinkling the cheese and crumb topping just before baking.

Prep time: 20 mins
Cooking time: 6 mins   *Bridget Turner*
Serves 4   *London*

VEGETARIAN CASSEROLE

2 oz butter
2 aubergines
2 small onions
2 cloves garlic
4 small courgettes
1 tblsp cream
1 tsp oregano
1 tsp salt

6 oz cooked chopped spinach
4 tomatoes
ground black pepper
1 oz marg
1 oz flour
½ pint milk
4 oz cheddar cheese

Scour the aubergines, sprinkle with salt and leave to stand for about 20 mins. Chop finely the onions and garlic, fry in a little butter until cooked, set aside. Slice the aubergines and courgettes and cook them separately in the remaining butter. Place the slices of aubergines mixed with half the onions and garlic on the bottom of a casserole, cover with spinach and cream. Lay slices of tomatoes over this, and make another layer with the courgettes and remaining onion and garlic. Season with oregano, pepper and salt. Now make a cheese sauce with the final ingredients. Melt marg in a pan, mix in the flour and gradually add the milk. Stir in grated cheese and continue to cook for a few mins before pouring this over the vegetables. Place casserole in a preheated oven at Gas mark 4, 350°F, 180°C, for 15-20 mins before serving.

Prep time: 3-4 hours
Cooking time: 20 mins
Serves 4

Sandra Macpherson of Glentruim
Newtonmore

LEEK AND MUSHROOM CRUMBLE

1 lb leeks
1 oz butter
2 tsp Dijon mustard
4 oz double cream

½ lb mushrooms (in season, field
    mushrooms are best)
4 tblsp cider (or dry white wine)
4 beaten eggs

Wash the leeks and slice thinly. Slice the mushrooms thinly. Put the butter, cider and mustard into a pan and heat until the butter has melted. Bring to a gentle boil and add the leeks and mushrooms, cover and cook gently for 5 mins. Allow to cool before mixing in the eggs and cream. Season to taste.

The crumble topping:

3 oz wholemeal flour
2 oz butter
3 oz porridge oats

2 tblsp oil
s and p

In a bowl rub the butter into the flour. Add the porridge oats and stir in the oil. Season to taste. Fill a shallow casserole with the leek and mushroom mixture and spread the crumble topping over it. Bake at Gas mark 5, 375°F, 190°C, for 35 mins. Serve hot with a winter or green salad, for lunch or supper.

Prep time: 5 mins
Cooking time: 40 mins
Serves 4

Peter and Marjorie Bourne
Aberfeldy

LEEK PIE

½ lb shortcrust pastry (wholemeal is nicest)
1 lb leeks, trimmed and washed (the only way to clean leeks is to split them lengthways down the middle and rinse)

½ lb white sauce made with:
3 oz butter
3 oz flour
½ pint milk
6 oz grated cheese
s and p

Make pastry and leave in cool place for at least 1 hour. Cut leeks into small slices and cook gently in 4 tblsp water until tender but not mushy. Drain, add leeks, cheese and s and p to sauce. Roll out pastry, line 9″ flan case, fill with leek mixture and sprinkle grated cheese on top. Bake in hot oven, Gas mark 6, 400°F, 205°C, for about 30 mins or until golden on top. Delicious with crispy bacon – you can make this a more exotic dish by adding things to sauce, e.g. egg yolks, cream, wine or all 3.

Prep time: 30 mins
Cooking time: 30 mins
Serves 4-6

Sonia Yellowlees
Aberfeldy

BUTTER BEAN AND LEEK PIE

4 oz butter beans
2 oz marg
8 oz carrots
4 oz mushrooms
8 oz tinned tomatoes

¼ pint stock
s and p
1 lb leeks
1 tblsp flour

For pie crust:
8 oz puff pastry

beaten egg to glaze

Soak, drain and rinse the butter beans, cook until tender and drain. Preheat oven to Gas mark 7, 425°F, 220°C. Melt the marg in a fair sized pan, and put in the cleaned and sliced carrots, cover and cook very gently for 10 mins. Do not allow to brown. Add cleaned and sliced leeks and sliced mushrooms and cook for a further 10 mins. Sprinkle flour over the vegetables and stir to mix. Add tomatoes and stock and cook gently for a further 2-3 mins, stirring until thickened. Add the butter beans and season with s and p. Turn the mixture into a 2 pint pie dish and cool. Roll out the pastry and cover pie dish with it. Pinch the edges and brush surface with beaten egg, leaving a hole in the centre for steam to escape. Bake in preheated oven for 20 mins, reduce heat to Gas mark 5, 375°F, 190°C, for a further 15 mins. Serve with potatoes and a green salad.

Prep time: 40 mins
Cooking time: 35 mins *Kirsty Crerar*
Serves 4 *Perth*

'HEY PESTO!'

1 small jar pesto (basil sauce)
1 large onion, chopped
½ lb mushrooms, chopped
butter or vegetable oil
wholemeal pasta spirals
 (enough for 4)

4 oz can tomatoes
2 dessertsp tomato purée
pinch of mixed herbs
1 level dessertsp brown sugar
4-5 oz mature cheddar cheese

Cook spirals in boiling salted water for about 20 mins. Meanwhile sauter onions in a little butter or vegetable oil in a large pan, when tender add the pesto and heat through. When cooked add the spirals and mix well. Add the mushrooms and tomatoes, bring to a simmer and then add tomato purée, herbs, 3 oz cheese and sugar. Allow to simmer for about 10 mins, season to taste. More liquid may be needed and just add enough water to simmer in oven. Transfer the ingredients into a casserole dish and top with rest of cheese. Put into the oven for 20 mins, Gas mark 4, 340°F, 170°C, and if liked pop under grill for a few mins to give a crisp golden topping. Delicious served with green salad and garlic bread.

Prep time: 10 mins
Cooking time: 50-60 mins *Sunny Ormonde*
Serves 4 *Chester*

DANISH FLAN

6 oz S R flour	1 onion
2 oz marg	clove garlic
milk	14 oz tin tomatoes
8 rashers bacon	4 oz cheese
1 oz lard	1 tsp cornflour

Rub flour and marg together. Bind with milk and mix to a dough. Roll on to a flan dish. Chop bacon and onion and brown together with crushed garlic, in lard. Add tomatoes and simmer to a pulp. Mix tsp cornflour in a little cold water and add to mixture to thicken. Pour on to pastry and cook at Gas mark 6, 400°F, 205°C, for about 20 mins until slightly golden. Grate cheese on top and put back in oven until melted.

Prep time: 20 mins
Cooking time: 20-30 mins
Serves 2-3

Seonaid Hastie Smith
Moulin

VEGETABLE MACARONI

1 14 oz tin tomatoes	1 bay leaf
1 dessertsp tomato purée	1 tsp oregano
1 large aubergine	1 tsp sugar
2 cloves garlic	4 oz macaroni
3 courgettes	*For cheese sauce:* 2 oz marg
4 oz mushrooms	2 oz flour
1 large onion	1 pint milk
s and p	4 oz cheese

Wash and slice aubergine. Sprinkle with salt and leave for 20 mins. Prepare and slice other veg. Crush garlic. Fry onion and garlic lightly then add other veg. Sauter for approx 5 mins. Add tomatoes, herbs, tomato purée, sugar, s and p and simmer until veg are soft. Boil macaroni until tender and make up cheese sauce. Mix all ingredients together. This mixture is best left for a few hours off the heat to allow the flavours to blend, but can be served immediately. Another suggestion is to pour it into an ovenproof dish and sprinkle with a mixture of grated cheese and breadcrumbs and brown under the grill. It is a lovely lunch or supper dish and could be served with garlic or herb bread and/or a crisp green salad.

Prep time: 30 mins
Cooking time: 20 mins
Serves 4-6

Di Barbour
Dunkeld

HOT BULGAR WITH CORIANDER

8 oz bulgar	3 level tsp chopped parsley
2 level tsp chopped fresh coriander	8 tblsp light stock
11½ oz can sweetcorn, drained	s and p
1 oz butter	

Soak bulgar in a bowl in cold water to cover to 1 cm above bulgar for 30 mins. Drain. Using ½ butter, lightly grease a shallow ovenproof dish. Put bulgar in dish and stir in all other ingredients, pouring over stock last with remaining butter, grease a large piece of greaseproof paper, cover dish tightly, and then with foil. Bake at Gas mark 4, 350°F, 180°C, for about 45 mins. Fork through lightly before serving.

To freeze:
Prepare until ready for oven, but do not cook. To use, thaw out at room temperature overnight and cook as above.

Prep time: 35 mins
Cooking time: 45 mins *Barbara Liddell*
Serves 6-8 *Pitlochry*

BULGAR VEGETABLE SAVOURY

6 oz bulgar	¾ pint boiling water
1 level tsp yeast extract	1 tblsp sunflower oil
1 med onion, sliced	1 stick celery, finely sliced
1 carrot, finely sliced	1 leek, finely sliced
2 level tblsp chopped parsley	2 tomatoes, skinned and chopped
½ level tsp paprika	s and p

Cook bulgar in the boiling water with yeast extract for about 10 mins until water has been absorbed. Heat oil in large pan and sauter onion, celery, carrot and leek for 10 mins, till lightly browned. Stir in bulgar, season and add 1 tblsp parsley, tomatoes and paprika. Serve in individual bowls, sprinkled with remaining parsley. Serve as a side dish with meat, or as a main dish.

Time: 1 hour *Barbara Liddell*
Serves 6 *Pitlochry*

ITALIAN HOT VEGETABLE MOUSSE

8 oz cooked peas	10 fl oz cooked thick white sauce
8 oz cooked spinach	2 oz grated Parmesan cheese
2 whole beaten eggs	5 rashers grilled back bacon
s and p	

Chop vegetables and bacon in blender to a pulp, add white sauce and beaten eggs. Add Parmesan and beat well so that mixture is fully blended. Pour into a buttered ovenproof dish (a souffle dish would do well) and cook in oven at Gas mark 3, 340°F, 170°C, for 25 mins – or microwave for 8 mins on full power, until set.

Prep time: 30 mins
Cooking time: 20-25 mins   *Louisa Ramazzotti*
Serves 4-6   *Enochdhu*

STUFFED CABBAGE LEAVES

1 savoy cabbage	seasoning to taste
1 small onion	1 oz marg
1 clove garlic	1 oz flour
6 oz mushrooms	½ pint milk
2 oz red and green peppers	4 oz cheddar cheese
1½ oz butter	2 oz sweetcorn
4 oz cooked rice	

Cook the cabbage leaves whole and allow to cool once they are strained. Chop finely the onion, garlic, peppers and mushrooms. Fry them gently in the butter until cooked, stir in the sweetcorn and cooked rice. Season to taste. Melt the marg and mix in the flour, gradually adding the milk to make a thick sauce. Grate cheese into the sauce and continue to cook for a few mins, season to taste. Add a little of the cheese sauce to the prepared filling combining these ingredients together. Place the mixture on top of four to eight cabbage leaves and roll them up. Lay these in a greased ovenproof dish and pour remaining cheese sauce over the top. heat in an oven preheated at Gas mark 4, 350°F, 180°C, for 15 mins before serving.

Prep time: 30 mins
Cooking time: 15 mins   *Sandra Macpherson of Glentruim*
Serves 4   *Newtonmore*

BAKED BEANS

1 lb pinto beans (from health food shop)	2 onions, finely sliced
	6 tblsp tomato sauce or ketchup
2 tsp salt	2 tblsp vinegar
6 tblsp syrup	a dash of tabasco
1 tsp dry mustard	

Cover beans with water and bring to the boil. Boil 2 mins. Remove from heat and allow to soften and swell one hour. Add sliced onion and season to taste. Return pan to heat, bring to boil and simmer until tender, approx 1 to 1½ hours. Add more liquid if necessary. Preheat oven to Gas mark 3, 325°F, 156°C. When beans are tender, drain, reserving ¾ pint liquid. Combine with all other ingredients. Put beans in casserole and pour liquid on top. Cover and bake in oven for 1½ hours. Uncover and bake for a further hour. This freezes well, and although the cooking time is long it can be done with other baking to share the oven and is much tastier than the tinned kind.

Time: 4 hours   *Ann Maxwell*
Serves 8 or more   *Pitlochry*

VEGETARIAN TOAD-IN-THE-HOLE

4 oz lentils   *For the batter:*
1 onion   4 oz S R wholewheat flour
1 clove garlic   ½ tsp s and p
4 oz mushrooms   2 eggs
1 tsp thyme   ½ pint milk
4 tblsp oil

Wash and soak lentils, rinse and cook till soft, then drain them. Preheat oven to Gas mark 7, 425°F, 220°C. Heat 2 tblsp oil in a fair sized saucepan and fry chopped onion and crushed garlic for 5 mins until lightly brown. Add mushrooms and cook a further 5 mins. Stir in the thyme, lentils, s and p to taste. Keep mixture hot. Put the remaining oil in a baking tin in the oven and make the batter. Put the wholewheat flour and ½ tsp salt into a bowl – make a well in the centre, and add the eggs and about ⅓ of the milk. Beat with a wooden spoon or with a hand mixer till thoroughly mixed, gradually adding rest of milk. Pour the batter straight into hot fat in pan in oven, and then spoon lentil mixture on top. Bake for 20-25 mins until risen and golden. Serve with gravy, potatoes and vegetables.

Prep time: 40 mins
Cooking time: 20-25 mins   *Kirsty Crerar*
Serves 4-6   *Perth*

CASSEROLE OF AUBERGINES

3 med aubergines   8 oz cheddar cheese, grated
Sauce:
1 onion   1 stalk celery
1 x 14oz tin tomatoes   s and p
bay leaf   little sugar

Slice aubergines, sprinkle with salt and drain for 1 hour. Dry with a paper towel. Meanwhile fry the chopped onion, add the chopped celery, then the tomatoes and bay leaf, sugar and seasoning. Simmer for 30 mins. Put alternate layers of aubergines, cheese and tomato sauce in an ovenproof dish, top with cheese and bake at Gas mark 4, 350°F, 175°C, for 1½ hours. Delicious as a supper dish or with cold meat.

Prep time: 15 mins
Cooking time: 2 hours   *Jennifer King*
Serves 4   *Aberfeldy*

THANKS

Thank God for dirty dishes
They have a tale to tell
While others may go hungry
We're eating very well.
With home, health and happiness
I shouldn't want to fuss,
By the stack of evidence,
God's been very good to us.

Mrs Ferguson
North Carolina

Chapter 5

SAVOURIES –
SAUCES – CHUTNEY

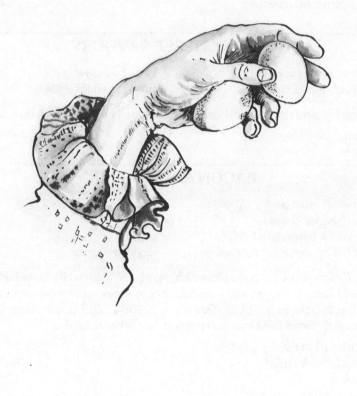

TORTA DI BLEIA OR OMELETTE VERTE

1 teacup cooked spinach   6 well beaten eggs
3 oz grated Parmesan cheese   s and p
6 oz minced raw beef, or cooked ham

Well drain and finely chop the spinach and fold it quite gently into the well beaten eggs. Stir in the cheese and the meat and season with s and p. Tip the mixture into a generously buttered straight-sided earthenware pot, or a loaf tin. Cover with a lid or foil and bake fairly low down in the oven, Gas mark 2, 310°F, 150°C, until the mixture is just set and slightly springy, when you press the top. Leave until cold and turn out. Splendid made for a picnic, when you want to arouse comment, such as, "Whatever is it?", "How unusual and how delicious." Vegetarians could omit the meat and increase the cheese. When no spinach is available, I have used leaves of the dreaded weed ground elder, which tastes similar.

Prep time: 15 mins
Cooking time: 60 mins   *Maggie Thorburn*
Serves 8   *Enochdhu*

QUICK CHEESE SAVOURY

½ pint double cream   1 crushed clove garlic
finely chopped chives   grated cheddar cheese

Whip cream, add other ingredients. Place in small heaps on savoury biscuits.

Prep time: 10 mins   *Bobby Campbell-Preston*
Serves 8   *Connel*

BACON AND EGG PIE

4 oz short crust pastry   ¼ tsp dry mustard
3 oz cheddar cheese   2 eggs
1 small tin evaporated milk   parsley
3 oz bacon rashers, chopped   sliced tomatoes

Line a 7" flan tin or deep pie plate with pastry and prick well – bake blind. Beat eggs, add bacon, cheese and mustard. Stir in evaporated milk, and pour into pastry case. Bake in hot oven, Gas mark 7, 400°F, 205°C, for about 40 mins. Garnish with sliced tomatoes and parsley. Serve hot or cold.

Prep time: 10 mins
Cooking time: 40 mins   *Sheila Keith*
Serves 4-6   *Pitlochry*

DOLCELATTE CHEESE PUFFS

Filo pastry: It's a great standby, and freezes well. Can be bought from a good delicatessan and from it you can create fantastic savouries and very light apple strudels.

Unthaw the Filo pastry and cut each length into small squares. Brush each layer of the squares with melted butter and place four layers on each square. Put a small piece of dolcelatte cheese on each square and bring the opposite corners together to meet at the top. Press together and seal. Pull together the other two corners to the top and seal. Brush again with melted butter and place on a baking sheet, Gas mark 7, 400°F, 205°C, for 10 mins. Serve hot, with cranberry sauce.

Prep time: 15-30 mins
Cooking time: 10 mins

Caroline Stroyan
Edinburgh

SMOKED TROUT SURPRISE

1 boned fillet of smoked trout per person	Filo pastry
melted butter	hollandaise sauce
whipped cream	chopped capers
chopped dill	

Make sure that the fish is free of bones. Unthaw the Filo pastry and brush each sheet with melted butter. Roll each fillet separately making about three layers of the pastry round it. Lay on a baking tray and brush with melted butter. Cook in the oven, Gas mark 7, 400°F, 205°C, for 7-10 mins. Serve with hollandaise sauce into which you have added whipped cream, some chopped capers and chopped dill. The sauce need only be warm.

Prep time: 15 mins
Cooking time: 7-10 mins

Caroline Stroyan
Edinburgh

CAMEMBERT CHEESE BALLS

Take a triangle of ripe Camembert cheese, egg and breadcrumb it – quickly fry in deep fat – serve with a sauce of gooseberry purée.

Prep time: depends on how many you make
Cooking time: 2 or 3 mins
Serves as many as you need

Caroline Stroyan
Edinburgh

QUICK SUPPER DISH

1 small can sweetcorn	grated cheese (to taste)
2 handfuls med oatmeal	1 egg
s and p	butter

Mix drained sweetcorn, oatmeal, and s and p and cheese with well beaten egg. Allow to stand for 15 mins, for oatmeal to soak up some of surplus liquid. Heat butter in a frying pan and make 4 patties with the mixture – turning when nicely browned underneath, to brown other side. Serve hot as they are, as a savoury or for a quick supper dish with hot crispy bacon and a green salad.

Prep time: 20 mins   *Barbara Liddell*
Serves 2   *Pitlochry*

CHEESE TARTLETS

4 oz grated cheese	1 oz butter
1 oz plain flour	½ pint milk
2 large eggs	salt and cayenne pepper
puff pastry	

Line 12-18 patty tins with thinly rolled out pastry. Melt butter in pan, stir in flour, add milk and boil for 3-4 mins, stirring continuously. Cool mixture and then stir in yolks. Cook gently for 2 or 3 mins, do not boil. Add cheese and season to taste, then stir in lightly the stiffly whisked egg whites. Fill cases and bake in quick oven, Gas mark 5-6, 380°F, 195°C, for about 20 mins, till risen and lightly browned. These make a good savoury, or as a nice change for coffee mornings.

Prep time: 20 mins
Cooking time: 20 mins   *Barbara Kirkwood*
Makess 12-18   *Bridge of Cally*

PIZZAS

For two bases:

1 lb cooked potatoes	1 lb S R flour
2 tsp salt	2 tsp powdered mustard
6 ozs butter	2 grated onions

Mix together the ingredients; adding enough milk to make a soft dough. Halve, and place on baking trays, moulding to 9″ circles.

For a salami pizza (with one base):

14 oz can drained tomatoes	6 oz gouda cheese
pinch dried basil	6 oz sliced cheese
oil	black olives for decoration
6 oz sliced salami	

Top first base with drained tomatoes, basil and gouda cheese. Brush with oil and bake for 25 mins at Gas mark 6-7, 400°F, 205°C. Then cover with salami and sliced cheese. Decorate with olives, brush with oil and return to oven for 5 mins.

For sardine or pilchard pizza:
Read fish for salami, and proceed as above.

Prep time: 15-20 mins
Cooking time: 25 mins
Each will serve 4

Sybil Currie
Pitlochry

ASPARAGUS AND CORN FLAN

8″ flan case filled with cooked shortcrust pastry shell	1 oz marg
	1 oz plain flour
1 can asparagus 'cuts'	½ pint liquid (from 2 cans
1 can sweetcorn	with milk added)
1 hard-boiled egg	s and p

Put drained asparagus and corn into pastry case. Chop hard-boiled egg, scatter over asparagus and corn. Make a well seasoned sauce with the marg, flour and liquid. Pour sauce over the flan. Serve hot or cold. Cheese may be used as a garnish. *Made as individual tartlets, this recipe is a good starter.*

Prep time: 5 mins
Serves 4

Sheila Turner
Pitlochry

NEVER FAIL
HOLLANDAISE SAUCE

4 egg yolks
2 tblsp lemon juice
4 oz unsalted butter
¼ tsp s and p

dash cayenne pepper
2 oz boiling water
(2 oz tarragon vinegar may be
    used instead of lemon juice)

Beat the egg yolks and lemon juice and vinegar together with a wooden spoon in the top of a double boiler. Add third of the butter. Stir constantly until the mixture starts to thicken. Remove from the heat and add second third of the butter, and stir rapidly. Add remaining butter and stir until all is completely blended. Add s and p and boiling water. Return to double boiler and stir until desired consistency. This never fails – and may be reheated.

Prep time: 5 mins
Cooking time: 10 mins

Norah Douglas
Binbrook

ITALIAN TOMATO SAUCE, FOR SPAGHETTI OR PASTA

2 tins Italian peeled, plum tomatoes
    (14 oz tins)
1 large courgette
1 celery stick
3 fl oz olive oil

1 bay leaf
1 carrot
1 med onion
s and p
1 squirt tomato paste

Chop onion and celery and roughly grate the carrot and courgette. Put these 4 ingredients in a casserole with the olive oil, and stir fry until the vegetables are soft. Add bay leaf, and s and p. Turn the gas up a little and add the 2 tins of tomatoes and their juices, stir well and bring to the boil. Cook on moderate heat for 1 hour. The sauce must simmer, but not boil, so that it reduces slightly, and all the flavours blend. Before serving discard the bay leaf, and adjust the salt. Add the tomato paste. When used with pasta, don't forget to add grated Parmesan cheese on the pasta!

Prep time: 20 mins
Cooking time: 1 hour
Serves 4-5

Louisa Ramazzotti
Enochdhu

PORK SPARE RIB SAUCE

1½ tsp salt
½ tsp pepper (black)
2 tblsp ground coriander seed
2 tblsp ground cumin seed
2 med sized chopped onions

1 tsp ground ginger
½ cup of soft dark brown sugar
½ cup salad oil
½ cup soya sauce
½ cup of lemon or lime juice

Liquidise all ingredients until smooth, put in a saucepan and bring to boil. Boil for about 15 mins. Use as a side sauce for roast spare ribs. This will keep indefinitely in a screwtop jar in the fridge.

Prep time: 10 mins
Cooking time: 15 mins

Mary Liddell
Pitlochry

SPAGHETTI SAUCE

5 peeled tomatoes
1 med onion
oil for cooking

2 or 3 rashers streaky bacon
1 clove garlic, chopped

Cook bacon in a little oil, on a low flame, till cooked and crisp. Add chopped onion and cook till golden brown. Add garlic and tomatoes and cook very slowly, for 10 mins. Serve with spaghetti or pasta, with Parmesan cheese.

Prep time: 5 mins
Cooking time: 15 mins

Anon.

MAYONNAISE

1 tin Carnation milk
1 breakfast cup white malt vinegar
1 breakfast cup granulated sugar

3 eggs (added last)
½ tsp salt
½ tsp dry mustard

Put vinegar, sugar, salt and mustard in a pan, and melt down before boiling. Then add Carnation milk and cook for a few minutes. Add well beaten eggs to mixture and beat well till not quite boiling. Cool mixture and then pour into jam jars. Keeps well, for months.

Time: 15 mins
Makes 3 x 1 lb jars

Betty Innes
Perth

BASIC MAYONNAISE

1 large egg
¼ pint veg oil
1 large tsp olive oil
2 tblsp white wine vinegar
    or lemon juice

1 large tsp sugar
1 large tsp salt
1 large tsp dried mustard
yoghourt

In blender put one whole egg. Whisk with sugar, salt and dried mustard. Add ½ corn oil, whisking all the time, then olive oil, then vinegar or lemon juice – then add rest of oil to make a very thick consistency. keep in a jar in fridge. When needed, add ½ mayonnaise to ½ yoghourt to make amount of mayonnaise required. basic mix keeps well in fridge for 2-3 weeks.

Time: 10 mins

Margo Ross
Pitlochry

AUSTRALIAN MAYONNAISE

½ tin condensed milk
½ cup vinegar
¼ cup oil (vegetable, sunflower or peanut)

1 egg yolk
2 tsp mixed mustard
s and p

Put all ingredients in a jar, and shake well, for 5 mins. This is delicious and keeps well in fridge.

Prep time: 10 mins
No cooking

Jean Tregarthen
Sydney

SALAD DRESSING I

1 small chopped onion
1 tblsp salad oil

3 tblsp vinegar
3 tblsp castor sugar

Mix all together and let it stand for a few hours before using. This keeps for a long time if well corked. Shake it well before using.

Prep time: 5 mins
No cooking

Jean Robertson
Dunkeld

SALAD DRESSING II

6 raw eggs
1 tsp salt
1 tsp dry mustard
½ teacup sugar

8 oz melted butter
1 tsp pepper
2 teacups malt vinegar

Beat all together thoroughly, and heat in a saucepan, stirring constantly until it thickens like boiled custard. But don't let it boil, or it will curdle and be spoiled. Bottle when cold. To prepare for table – thin down with milk and add more sugar to taste.

Prep time: 10 mins
Cooking time: 10-15 mins

Peggy Bruges
Dunkeld

PINEAPPLE-ORANGE SAUCE

6 tblsp brown sugar
½ tblsp cornflour
1 cup water
1 cup orange juice

grated rind of 1 orange
⅓ cup crushed pineapple
¼ cup raisins

Combine ingredients in the order listed omitting raisins. Heat to boiling and cook for 3 mins. Add ¼ cup raisins and cook till they puff up. Serve with ham or tongue.

Prep time: 5 mins
Cooking time: 5 mins

Mary Cairncross
Perth

HOT CHOCOLATE FUDGE SAUCE (MICROWAVE)

1 oz butter
2 level tsp cocoa
1 level tsp vanilla

3 oz soft brown sugar
2 level tsp milk

Melt butter in glass bowl or dish for 1 minute. Stir in other ingredients and cook uncovered for 2 mins. Stir well. Pour hot over ice-cream. Can be served with hot sponge pudding, or cool, spooned over profiteroles.

Prep time: 5 mins
Cooking time: 3 mins
Serves 6-8

Hazel Barbour
Fincastle

APPLE CHUTNEY

2 lb apples, cut roughly	2 cloves garlic, crushed
¾ lb brown sugar	2 large onions, chopped
¾ lb sultanas	1 pint malt vinegar
½ oz salt	½ oz ginger
¼ oz mustard seed	

Simmer vinegar, sugar, apples and onions gently until reduced to pulp. Stir in remaining ingredients. When well mixed, turn into bowl and stir 5 or 6 times while cooling. When cool, bottle and store. Very good with any cold meat and baked potatoes.

Prep time: 10 mins   *Douglas Hutchison, CBE, MC*
Cooking time: 15 mins   *Aberfeldy*

CURRIED FRUIT

20 oz can pear halves	¾ cup brown sugar
20 oz can peach halves	3-4 tsp curry powder
20 oz can pineapple rings	12 cherries
½ cup butter	

Arrange fruit in ovenproof dish (approx 12″ × 8″), decorate with cherries. Melt butter in pan, stir in brown sugar and curry powder then pour over fruit. Bake in mod oven, Gas mark 3, 325°F, 165°C, for 15-20 mins. Delicious with any cold meat dish – e.g. roast stuffed pork or ham.

Cooking time: 25 mins   *Elizabeth Hood*
Serves 10-12   *Pitlochry*

MINCEMEAT MADE WITH GREEN TOMATOES

3¾ lb green tomatoes	1¼ lb apples
½ lb seedless raisins	½ tblsp salt
½ cup Atora suet	¼ cup vinegar
½ tblsp cinnamon	½ tblsp ground cloves
¼ tblsp nutmeg	1 minced orange
1 minced lemon	

Chop, and then scald tomatoes twice. Add rest of ingredients. Boil for 2 hours until thick. Bottle and/or freeze. This freezes well.

Prep time: 20 mins   *Elizabeth Soutar*
Cooking time: 2¼ hours   *Broughty Ferry*

SPICED APPLE AND AUBERGINE CHUTNEY

3 lb cooking apples
(when peeled and cored)
1 lb aubergines
1½ pints vinegar
3 large onions
1 tsp mixed spice

1 lb soft brown sugar
s and p
6 oz sultanas
½ to 1 tsp cayenne
1-2 cloves garlic (optional)
1 tsp curry powder (optional)

Cut apples into small pieces. Slice washed aubergines (put salt on for 15 mins and wash and drain). Put apples, aubergines, seasoning, peeled and chopped onions and garlic into pan. Add enough vinegar to cover. Simmer gently for 30 mins, adding more vinegar if necessary to prevent mixture sticking. Stir in the rest of the ingredients until all the sugar has dissolved. You can put in 1 to 2 little red hot peppers, and pick out at end if liked. Boil steadily, stirring from time to time for another 30 mins till it looks like thick jam. Put into hot jars and seal down.

Prep time: 20 mins
Cooking time: 1 hour
Makes about 7 lbs

Mary Clare Agius
Ta'xbiex, Malta

UNCOOKED RELISH

7 lbs ripe tomatoes (blanched and peeled)
2 large bunches celery
6 large onions
2 red, 2 green peppers

½ cup salt
6 cups white sugar
2 cups cider vinegar

Chop finely tomatoes and celery. Add ½ cup salt, and leave to stand overnight. Drain the following morning. Chop red and green peppers and add to above mixture. To make syrup, add 6 cups white sugar to 2 cups cider vinegar and bring to boil. Pour hot syrup over vegetables and stir often through the day. Pour into hot sterilised jars in the evening.

Prep time: 15 mins
Makes 10 lbs

Elizabeth Hood
Pitlochry

HOW TO PRESERVE HUSBANDS:

Be careful in your selection. Do not choose too young. Once, when selected, give your entire thoughts to preparation for domestic use. Some insist on keeping them in a pickle – others are constantly getting them into hot water. This makes them sour, hard and sometimes bitter. Even poor varieties may be made sweet, tender and good, by garnishing them with patience, well seasoned with love, and sweetened with kisses. Wrap them in a mantle of charity. Keep warm with a steady, fine and domestic devotion, and serve with peaches and cream. Thus prepared, they will keep for years.

South African

Chapter 6

PUDDINGS

OLD CAPE BRANDY PUDDING

1 cup sugar	¼ lb butter
2 whisked eggs	salt
¼ tsp baking powder	1½ cups flour
½ cup chopped nuts	1 cup dates
1 tsp soda bicarb	1 cup boiling water

Cream butter, sugar, add eggs, salt, baking powder, flour and nuts. Boil dates in water with soda bicarb. Add to creamed mixture, stirring well. Pour into greased fireproof dish and bake for 35-40 mins, at Gas mark 5, 375°F, 190°C.

Syrup:

1¾ cups sugar	1 cup water
1 tblsp butter	1 tsp vanilla essence
¾ cup brandy	

Boil water, sugar and butter for 5 mins. Remove from heat, add vanilla essence and brandy. Pour over hot baked pudding. This may seem too much sauce, but use it all!

Prep time: 15 mins
Cooking time: 45 mins
Serves 8

Janetta Watters
Strathtay

SAGO PLUM PUDDING

4 tblsp sago or tapioca	3 oz breadcrumbs
1 breakfast cup milk	1 tblsp melted butter
½ tsp soda bicarb	4 oz sultanas
4 oz currants	3 oz sugar

Soak sago or tapioca in milk overnight. Next day add breadcrumbs, melted butter, soda bicarb, prepared fruit and sugar. Put into a greased, steamed pudding basin with lid and steam for 4 hours. It can also be cooked in a slow cooker on a high setting overnight. This is a good alternative to a rich Xmas pudding – it's very light, and good with cream or brandy butter.

Prep time: start night before plus 10 mins
Cooking time: 4 hours
Serves 6

Mary Liddell
Pitlochry

PLUM PUDDING

1½ lb Atora suet	½ lb candied peel
8 cloves	2 lb sultanas
¼ oz mace and cinnamon	1½ lb stoned raisins
pinch salt	2 lb moist brown sugar
juice of 2 lemons	rind of 3 lemons
1 glass port wine	¼ pint brandy
8-10 eggs, to make mixture a little	1½ lb breadcrumbs
wetter than a cake	1 heaped dessertsp plain flour

Mix all dry ingredients in a large bowl. Mix in the eggs, one or two at a time, add the brandy and port and stir very well. Put in 4 medium bowls, cover with greaseproof and foil and boil for 8 hours, or boil for 1½ to 2 hours and cook rest of time in a slow oven. Boil again for about 4 hours on the day.

Great-grandmother's recipe.

Prep time: 20 mins
Cooking time: 8 hours, and 4 hours day of use   *Daphne Berridge*
Makes 4 med puddings   *Dorchester*

PARTY BREAD AND BUTTER PUDDING

2 oz butter	6 oz seedless raisins (soaked
8 thin slices bread (decrusted)	overnight in 3 tblsp brandy)
4 oz apricot jam	3 large eggs, beaten with
2 oz castor sugar	2 extra yolks
½ pint rich milk	½ pint double cream
a few drops vanilla essence	

Butter a 9"-10" in diameter ovenproof dish (about 2" deep) scatter the soaked raisins evenly over dish. Butter the bread and make sandwiches with the apricot jam. Cut each slice into 4 pieces and place in dish. Beat eggs and extra yolks with sugar. Bring the milk, cream and vanilla slowly to the boil. Pour hot liquid into the egg mixture and whisk thoroughly. Pour this mixture over the bread and leave for 10 mins or more to soak in. Place dish in roasting tin, with cold water half way up sides of dish, being careful not to let any spill into pudding. Bake in a preheated oven, Gas mark 3, 320°F, 160°C for 45-60 mins or till custard is just set and bread lightly browned. Sprinkle with cup of sugar and serve with whipped cream.

Prep time: 25 mins
Cooking time: 45-60 mins   *Barbara Bassett-Smith*
Serves 6-8   *Strathtay*

FRUIT AND APPLE PUDDING WITH BUTTER SAUCE

½ lb short pastry
½ lb dried mixed fruit
½ teacup sugar
¼ tsp mixed spice

2 large cooking apples
4 oz butter
¼ tsp cinnamon

Preheat oven to Gas mark 4, 340°F, 170°C. Roll out the pastry on a floured board or surface, fairly thinly, or until you have approx 12″ × 16″ rectangle. Grate the apple on to the pastry and add the mixed dried fruit, spreading it over the apple. Add the spices by sprinkling them over the mixture. Then taking one end of the pastry, roll it up and seal the overlapping edge with milk or egg. Place on a baking sheet or ovenproof china dish. Cut the butter in cubes and place on top. Sprinkle the sugar all over this and then pour a cup of boiling water over it. Place in the oven on the middle shelf and bake for approx 40 mins – basting once or twice with its own juice. Serve hot with whipped cream – also delicious cold. The sauce makes itself during cooking time.

Prep time: 15 mins
Cooking time: 40 mins
Serves 6-8

Michael Pickworth
London

FAR BRETON

1¾ pints scalded milk
6 ozs sugar
approx 8 oz tinned or stewed prunes

6 oz flour
6 eggs

Use a large mixing bowl. Place sugar and flour in bowl. Make a well in centre, add the beaten eggs. Add the hot milk a little at a time, beating well. Mix very thoroughly. Place stoned prunes in a very well buttered shallow large casserole dish. Pour over the egg mixture. Bake in oven Gas mark 9, 490°F, 240°C, for 10 mins, reduce heat to Gas mark 4, 360°F, 180°C, for 1 hour 10 mins. Serve hot or cold with cream.

Prep time: 10 mins
Cooking time: 1 hr 20 mins
Serves 6

Elisabeth Soutar
Broughty Ferry

SYRUP SPONGE PUDDING (MICROWAVE)

This basic sponge recipe can be used with jam, marmalade, mixed fruit etc instead of syrup. Butter can be used instead of marg.

3 tblsp golden syrup
½ tsp baking powder
6 oz castor sugar

6 oz S R flour
6 oz soft marg
3 size-3 eggs

Grease a 2-pint pudding basin, and put syrup in it. Mix all other ingredients together thoroughly, till soft and fluffy. Pour sponge mixture carefully over syrup. Cover with cling film, making a slit in film with a sharp knife to prevent ballooning. Cook in microwave on full power for 6 minutes. When cooked, a skewer should come out cleanly. Allow to stand for 5 mins before serving.

Prep time: 5 mins
Cooking time: 6 mins and 5 mins resting
Serves 4

Nighean Ross
Pitlochry

URNEY PUDDING

2 eggs
2 oz butter
½ tsp baking soda

2 oz plain flour
1 oz sugar
a little jam

Put butter and sugar in basin and beat to a cream. Add eggs and beat smooth, mix soda with flour and fold into mixture, blending all thoroughly. Add jam. Pour into a buttered bowl, cover with greased paper and steam for 1½ hours. Turn out and serve with a hot sweet sauce. This is an exceptionally light steamed pudding.

Prep time: 10 mins
Cooking time: 1½ hours
Serves 4

Mavis Bowman Edgar
Ballinluig

FRENCH STRAWBERRY FLAN

8 oz shortcrust pastry
2 egg yolks

4 tblsp syrup
strawberries

Line a flan tin with pastry and bake blind for 10 mins, Gas mark 7, 425°F, 215°C. Melt syrup and beat in egg yolks. Pour into flan and bake 30 mins at Gas mark 4, 350°F, 175°C, until golden brown. Remove from oven and quickly cover top with whole or halved strawberries, pressing them down firmly. Serve warm with cream.

Prep time: 15 mins
Cooking time: 30 mins
Serves 6

Fiona Barron
Alyth

RASPBERRY SHORTBREAD

6 oz flour	½ tsp ground ginger
3½ oz moist brown sugar	1 tsp baking powder
2 oz butter	1 lb raspberries
2 tblsp castor sugar	

Put raspberries into a fairly shallow pie dish and scatter white sugar over them. Rub butter into flour, add sugar, ginger and baking powder. Spread this mixture over the fruit and smooth it out. Bake in the centre of an oven, Gas mark 4, 350°F, 175°C, for 25 mins. Eat hot or cold.

Time: 30-35 mins
Serves 4-6

Malize McBride
Aberfeldy

GYPSY TART

6-7 oz shortcrust pastry	6 oz soft brown sugar
1 small tin condensed milk	

Line a 7″ flan case with the pastry and bake blind for 25 mins on Gas mark 7, 425°F, 215°C. Mix milk and sugar together thoroughly with a fork. Pour into flan case and bake for 15-20 mins till set, on Gas mark 4, 350°F, 175°C.

Time: 1 hour
Serves 4-6

Elizabeth Steuart-Fothringham
Forfar

BANANA TART

Pastry:	*Filling:*
8 oz wheat flour	8 bananas
6 oz butter	2 eggs
3 oz sugar	5 oz sugar
1 egg	4 oz ground almonds
	1 lemon
	3 dessertsp rum

Use soft butter. Squeeze lemon juice, cut bananas into slices, cover with rum and half the lemon juice, dust with 1 oz sugar and leave to marinate.

Pastry: Put flour into a bowl and make a hole in the flour – to which the egg is added, with the sugar and butter in walnut sizes. Rub in with fingertips and make a ball with the paste. Grease a tart mould. Roll out paste until the thickness of a 2p piece and line mould. Prick pastry with fork and bake blind at, Gas mark 4, 350°F, 175°C, for 10-15 mins, or till pastry is brown.

Filling· Mix eggs with sugar and beat till creamy, then add ground almonds and the other half of lemon juice. Place banana slices in the tart case in circles to the centre of the dish. Add marinated liquid to the almond cream, and pour this over the bananas. Cook for 20-25 mins in a mod oven, Gas mark 4, 350°F, 175°C. Serve with cream.

Prep time: 20 mins
Cooking time: 15 mins and 25 mins
Serves 8

Karen Robinson
Eastleigh, Hants

BROWN SUGARED PEACHES WITH SOURED CREAM

4 large fresh peaches
½ level tsp powdered cinnamon
4 level tblsp castor sugar

2 level tblsp demerara sugar
½ pint soured cream

Heat grill before preparation. Dip peaches into boiling water, count 10 then plunge them into cold water. Skin, stone and slice peaches and arrange evenly in individual ovenproof dishes. Blend brown sugar with cinnamon and sprinkle over peaches. Spoon soured cream over them. Sprinkle each dish with 1 tblsp castor sugar and place under hot grill until sugar melts and caramelizes. A very hot grill is essential. Can be served hot or chilled.

Time: 20 mins
Serves 4

Anne Brown
Pitlochry

APFELKUCHEN

2 lb cooking apples
½ lb margarine
½ lb butter
approx ½ lb castor sugar

2 eggs
¾ lb self-raising flour
2 drops vanilla essence
½ tsp cinnamon

Put marg, butter, ¼ lb sugar and eggs in liquidiser. When liquidised, pour contents into a bowl with the flour, vanilla essence and cinnamon. Line a shallow baking dish with buttered greaseproof paper and spread the mixture into this dish. The mixture should be about ½" thick in a rectangular tin 12" × 8". Peel and core apples, quarter them and then cut into very thin ⅛" slices, and press them rounded side up into the mixture. Dredge the rest of the sugar over the top. Bake in a moderate hot oven, Gas mark 6, 400°F, 205°C, until apples are pale brown – about 1 hour. Eat hot as a pudding or cold as a cake.

Prep time: 20 mins
Cooking time: 1 hour
Serves 6-8

Mary Ogilvie
Kilry

SAUCER PANCAKES

2 oz plain flour   2 oz butter
2 oz castor sugar   2 eggs
½ pint milk   jam

Heat milk in a pan till warm. Cream butter and sugar till creamy, then beat in eggs and flour alternately. Add the warm milk, which may slightly curdle the mixture – but beat well, then cover and let it stand for about one hour. Grease 6 large saucers, put some batter in each (about ½-¾ fill each saucer) and bake quickly in oven, Gas mark 5, 375°F, 190°C, for 15-20 mins. Gently ease them off the saucers. put a dessertspoonful of jam on half of each pancake and flip the other half over. Serve with whipped cream.

Prep time: 10 mins plus 1 hour resting
Cooking time: 15-20 mins   *Barbara Liddell*
Serves 6   *Pitlochry*

CRUNCHIE PEARS

2 oz butter   2 oz soft brown sugar
4 oz fresh white breadcrumbs   2 oz walnuts or mixed nuts,
pinch of cinnamon   chopped
4 fresh pears, peeled and cored 4 dessertsp mincemeat

Melt butter in pan, add sugar, breadcrumbs, walnuts and cinnamon, and place pear halves in base of an ovenproof dish. Fill each pear half with a spoonful of mincemeat, and cover with breadcrumb topping. Bake in oven Gas mark 4, 350°F, 180°C, for 45 mins, and serve with whipped cream.

Prep time: 25 mins
Cooking time: 45 mins   *Iona Jamieson*
Serves 4   *Perth*

BRAMBLE FLAN

Rich shortcrust:
4 oz plain flour   brambles
2 oz fat   3 oz sugar
½ oz castor sugar   1 tsp cornflour
1 small egg yolk   whipped cream
mixed with ½ tblsp water   castor sugar
pinch salt

Make pastry as usual, line a flan tin and bake blind. Cook about ¼ lb brambles with 3 oz sugar and sieve. Fill flan case with whole new fruit. Thicken purée with 1 tsp cornflour and pour when boiling hot over raw fruit brushing a little over side of pastry. Cool and serve with whipped cream and castor sugar.

Prep time: 10 mins
Cooking time: 10 mins *Caroline Crawford*
Serves 4-5 *Blairgowrie*

EVERYONE'S FAVOURITE

Flan Case:
    4 oz butter or marg
    2 level tsp demerara sugar
    16 digestive biscuits, crushed

Filling:
    large can condensed milk
    ¼ pint double cream
    juice of 2 lemons (large)
    fruit to decorate

Melt butter or marg in pan, stir in sugar and biscuits. Mix well, and press into a large flan ring. Mix well in a bowl the condensed milk, cream and lemon juice and pour into flan case. Chill well. Decorate with mandarines, grapes or grated chocolate.

Time: 20-30 mins *Catriona Godson*
Serves 6-8 *Chiddingfold*

REFRIGERATOR LEMON CHEESECAKE

12 oz digestive biscuit crumbs
¼ oz gelatine
2 x 8 oz cartons cottage cheese

5-6 oz butter
8 tblsp lemon juice (2 lemons)
2 small tins Nestlé's milk

Make biscuit base with biscuit crumbs and melted butter. Melt gelatine in lemon juice in cup over hot water. Cool, and liquidise all the ingredients. Leave to cool until slightly thick. Pour over base and leave to set. Decorate with fresh fruit, e.g. strawberries, raspberries or pie filling.

Time: 20 mins *Katrina Liddell*
Serves 8 *Pitlochry*

VANILLA CHEESECAKE

Crust:
¾ pkt Rich Tea biscuits   ¼ lb butter

Filling:

1 lb cream cheese	¼ pint cream
2-4 tblsp sugar (to taste)	1 tsp vanilla essence
1 heaped dessertsp plain flour	pinch salt
2 eggs	

Crust: Melt butter and add finely crushed biscuits. Pat into base and sides of flan dish.

Filling: Mix filling ingredients all together, adding slightly beaten eggs last. Beat very well until smooth and creamy. Pour into biscuit shell. Bake in oven at Gas mark 2, 300°F, 150°C, for ½ hour. Should be firm to the touch. It firms up more as it cools. Serve slightly warm, freshly made. Do not overbake as this makes it leathery, and do not reheat.

Prep time: 15 mins
Cooking time: 30 mins   *Vivien Rossaak*
Serves 6   *Johannesburg*

SPICED APPLE CHEESECAKE

1 x 8 oz Philadelphia cheese	4 oz butter
¼ lb digestive biscuits	2 oz sultanas
½ lb carton apple purée	1 large spoon soft brown sugar
or 2 large cooking apples	¼ tsp each of cinnamon,
lemon juice	mixed spice
	chocolate

Melt half the butter, crumble the biscuits finely, butter an 8″ flan dish. Mix melted butter and crumbs and pat down firmly in flan dish and leave to cool. Put remaining butter into a saucepan, with the apple purée (or apples sliced thinly), sultanas, sugar and spices. Cook gently. Meanwhile cut cheese into 1″ cubes in mixing bowl. When apple mixture is soft, pour over cheese and mix thoroughly. Melt some dark chocolate and spread it over crumbs, reserve a small piece to grate over top. Spread apple and cheese mixture over chocolate and put in refrigerator to chill. Before serving decorate with grated chocolate.

Time: 25-30 mins   *Cecil Howman*
Serves 5-6   *Pitlochry*

PECAN MERINGUE

1 lb cracker biscuits
⅔ cup chopped pecan nuts
½ tsp baking powder
whipped cream and flake bar
   to decorate

3 egg whites
1 cup sugar
1 tsp vanilla essence

This you can make in less time than it takes to heat up your oven! Whip egg whites till stiff. Gradually add in sugar, then add baking powder and vanilla. Fold in crushed biscuits and nuts. Bake in a greased pie dish for ½ hour at Gas mark 4, 350°F, 175°C.

Prep time: very quick
Cooking time: 30 mins
Serves 4-6

Vivien Rossaak
Johannesburg

MARRON PAVLOVA

Meringue:
   3 egg whites
   ½ tsp vanilla essence
   1 tsp vinegar

6 oz castor sugar
1 tsp cornflour
pinch of salt

Heat oven to Gas mark 2, 300°F, 150°C. Line an 8″ tin with non-stick paper. Separate eggs, beat whites stiffly, add salt and beat in 3 oz of castor sugar. Mix cornflour with the rest of the sugar and fold in gently. Add vanilla and vinegar and mix lightly. Spread in tin and cook for one hour. Remove from oven and cool. Turn upside down and carefully remove paper.

Marron filling:
Spread the meringue base with contents of tin of marron or sweetened chestnut purée. Decorate with whipped cream.

Prep time: 15 mins
Cooking time: 1 hour
Serves 4-6

Angela Alexander
Callander

TAHITAN PAVLOVA

Using Pavlova base as previous recipe, continue with:

Filling:

½ pint double cream } whipped
½ pint single cream } together

15½ oz tin guavas, halved
1 lb 4 oz tin lychees, drained and stoned

Chop lychees and mix with ½ the cream. Pipe or spoon remaining cream round the pavlova base as above, about 1½" from the edge, and arrange guava petals over the cream. Pile lychees and cream mixture in the middle. Chill for ½ hour before serving.

Prep time: 15 mins
Cooking time: 1 hour
Serves 4-6

Deirdre Scott
Farnham

VICTORIAN CLARET JELLY

¾ bottle claret
¾ large cup currant or raspberry
  purée
½ oz gelatine

1 wineglass brandy
8 oz sugar
juice and rind of 1 lemon
whites and shells of 3 eggs

Put all these ingredients into a stewpan and whisk over heat until boiling. Simmer for 10 mins, strain through a muslin into a tube mould. Turn out when cold and fill the centre with cream, whipped with sugar, lemon juice and vanilla to taste.

Time: 40 mins
Serves 6-8

Eileen Cox
Dunkeld

Mrs Cox found this recipe in her grandmother's book, has tried it often and says it is definitely a dinner party sweet. The liquid measurements are vague, but so long as they measure about 2 pints all will be well.

PEARS A LA BORDELAISE

2 lbs pears
1 cup water
3½ oz castor sugar
1 or 2 drops vanilla
Garnish:
  ratafia biscuits
  redcurrant jelly

For the custard:
2 cups warm milk
vanilla pod
2 whole eggs and one yolk
3 oz castor sugar
1½ oz flour

Peel, core and halve the pears. Poach gently in the water to which you have added 3½ oz castor sugar and the vanilla essence. The pear halves must be tender but remain whole. For the custard, heat the milk with a small piece of vanilla pod which has been slit with a sharp knife to release the flavour even more. Beat 2 whole eggs and 1 yolk with 3 oz castor sugar and 1½ oz flour. Pour the warm milk on top, and thicken over a low heat until the custard coats the back of wooden spoon stirring all the time. To serve, pour the cooled custard into a dish, arrange the pear halves on top, sprinkle 3 or 4 crumbled ratafia biscuits on top and decorate with some redcurrant jelly. The pears should be Williams or Comice for best flavour.

Time: 50 mins   *Anna-Lise Robertson*
Serves 6   *Pitlochry*

STRAWBERRIES AND BANANAS WITH ORANGE MINT SAUCE

Strawberries and bananas, in ratio of 1 lb strawberries to 4 bananas. A sprig of mint, chopped into the juice of an orange. Just before serving crush strawberries, reserving a few large ones to garnish. Pour purée over chopped bananas, serve with cream and mint sauce – delicious!

Time: 10 mins   *Eileen Cox*
Serves 4   *Dunkeld*

NB: See hint on dealing with cut bananas in Household Hints Chapter.

NORWEGIAN CREAM

4 eggs   Tiptrees little scarlet strawberry jam
4 tblsp castor sugar   vanilla essence
1 pkt gelatine   2 tblsp water
cream

Separate eggs. Beat yolks until creamy with sugar. Add gelatine melted in the 2 tblsp water. Add a few drops of vanilla essence. Beat whites until stiff and fold into mixture. When set spread with jam and cover with whipped cream. Decorate with crushed biscuit crumbs.

Time: 30 mins   *Lady Kinnaird*
Serves 4-6   *Inchture*

AUSTRALIAN CREAM

walnuts for decoration
3 tblsp semolina
3 tblsp sugar

½ pint cream
4 teacups water
1 jelly

Put all ingredients into a pan, bring slowly to boil, stirring most of the time, and boil 3-4 mins. Beat in electric mixer for a few mins till light and fluffy or by hand for 20 mins. Pour into glass dish and decorate with whipped cream and chopped walnuts.

Time: 15 mins
Serves 5-6

Mary Rea
Aberfeldy

This sweet was a speciality in the 1920s.

CRUNCHY RASPBERRY AND PEAR CRUMBLE

2 level tsp cornflour
12 oz hulled raspberries
3 med sized pears peeled cored
    and sliced
4 oz plain flour

2 oz demerara sugar
3 oz granulated sugar
2 oz marg
1 oz crushed cornflakes

Mix cornflour, granulated sugar and raspberries. Arrange in layers with the pears in a greased 2-pint ovenproof dish. Sieve flour, rub in fat, stir in demerara sugar and crushed cornflakes, spoon over fruit, flatten with the back of a spoon. Cook at Gas mark 5, 375°F, 190°C, for 25 mins, reduced to Gas mark 4, 350°F, 175°C, for a further 15-20 mins till topping is golden and fruit tender. Serve hot or cold with custard or cream.

Prep time: 15 mins
Cooking time: 45 mins
Serves 4

Ann Duffy
Pitlochry

BABY ECLAIRS

4 fl oz hot water
equal volume of plain flour
pinch of salt
chocolate

1 oz butter
2 eggs
whipping cream

Melt the butter in the hot water, add the salt and bring to boil vigorously. Lift the pan off the heat, add all the flour at once, holding the saucepan over but not in contact with the hotplate. Beat the mixture together, using a wooden spoon, until the dough forms a single ball, clean from the sides of the pan. (This may sound improbable, but it is quick and easy, and is in fact what happens.) Remove the pan away from the heat, add the eggs one at a time, beating each one well in. Put ½ teaspoon of the batter on a greased baking sheet, well spaced as they will puff to perhaps 4 times their uncooked size. Cook at Gas mark 8, 440°F, 225°C, for at least 25 mins, depending on the size of the éclairs. They are cooked when they are puffed, golden brown and there are no little moisture bubbles to be seen on the surface. This quantity will make up to 50 profiteroles, and if you use this amount to make fewer than about 15 you will have great difficulty in cooking the éclairs satisfactorily, so that they stay puffed and hollow when cool.

To fill: When cold, split and fill with sweetened whipped cream. They can then be iced with chocolate or coffee flavoured water icing. Alternatively add a piece of soft fruit to the cream and dust with icing sugar. In winter they can be filled with a savoury cheese sauce and served hot as an accompaniment to drinks before dinner.

Time: 35 mins to make and bake, and ages to fill!   *Merril Sylvester*
Makes 50 profiteroles   *Aberfeldy*

CHERRY BRULEE

1 tin black stoned cherries   ½ pint cream
castor sugar

Place drained cherries in flan dish. Whip cream very stiff. Spread over cherries and deep freeze till solid. (About 1 hour.) Take out and cover with layer of sugar. Put under grill to melt and brown sugar. Replace in deep freeze. Take out about 1 hour before required.

Time: quick, except for chilling time   *Barbara Bassett-Smith*
Serves 4   *Strathtay*

RASPBERRY BRULEE

1 lb fresh raspberries   1 pint double cream
4 rounded tblsp demerara sugar

Place raspberries in a heatproof shallow china dish. Whisk cream until stiff, spread over fruit to cover and level the top. Chill for several hours until cream is firm. Sprinkle the sugar over evenly and place under hot grill, just long enough to melt the sugar and the surface is caramelised. Replace in fridge and chill again until the sugar becomes quite crisp.

Prep time: quick, except for chilling time   *The Countess of Strathmore*
No cooking   *Glamis*

LEMON CREAMS

8 egg yolks   5 oz sugar
juice and rind of 2 lemons   ½ pint cream

Beat egg yolks and sugar together, add lemon juice and rind, fold in cream. A
good recipe if you are making a large batch of meringues. *Own invention.*

Time: 10 mins   *Rosemary Mackenzie Ross*
Serves 8   *Inveresk*

ALMOND CASES

2 oz butter   2 oz ground almonds
2 oz castor sugar

Cream butter and sugar. Add ground almonds, put a good tspful into each patty
tin. Bake in a cool oven, Gas mark 2, 300°F, 150°C, for 10 mins. The mixture
will puff up and then sink down forming 'pastry' cases. Cool and fill with
steamed apple – or any other fruit – and top with whipped cream.

Prep time: 5 mins
Cooking time: 10 mins   *Hetta M'Gowan*
Serves 6   *Pitlochry*

BRAMBLE CREAMS

1 lb brambles   ¼ pint water
4 oz sugar   1 tblsp lemon juice
½ oz gelatine   ½ pint double cream

Stew brambles in water and sugar till tender. Taste for sweetness, adding more
sugar if required. Sieve while still warm into a basin. While brambles are
cooking, dissolve gelatine in 2 tblsp water and place over a pan of hot water till
melted. Add to bramble mixture. When mixture starts to set, stir in cream and
lemon juice, which have been whipped together till thick. Pour into individual
dishes and serve chilled. Place 4 or 5 whole brambles in centre of dish.

Time: 30 mins   *Isobel Mackinlay*
Serves 6   *Dullatur*

STRAWBERRY SNOW

strawberries   ½ pint double cream
whites of 2 eggs   2 oz castor sugar
sweet sherry   lemon juice

Chop the strawberries. Beat cream until thick. In a separate bowl beat egg whites until stiff, then fold into the cream. Add the sugar, lemon juice and sherry to taste. Fold most of the strawberries in to the mixture and gently stir in. Put it all into a serving dish and decorate with remaining strawberries.

Time: 10 mins   *Jenny Abramsky*
Serves 4-5   *London*

SNOW PUDDING

4 eggs   1 vanilla pod or ½ tsp vanilla essence
1 pint milk   Dash rum or brandy
6 oz sugar

Separate yolks from whites of eggs. Beat whites *very* stiffly. Add sugar and vanilla to milk and bring to boil. Poach the egg whites in the milk as follows: Take a generous tblsp of egg whites and place in the *simmering* milk. When the whites swell turn them and cook for a moment longer. Usually 3 tblsp of egg whites can be cooked at the same time. Place these carefully in the serving dish and continue until all whites have been used. Beat yolks thoroughly and add to the *cooled* milk. Strain into a bowl over a pan of hot water (or double boiler and cook carefully, stirring constantly until custard thickens). Sweeten and add a dash of brandy or rum. When cool pour custard round the islands of egg whites.

Time: 30-35 mins   *Charlotte Bingham*
Serves 6-8   *Pitlochry*

FLOATING ISLAND

For caramel:
4 oz castor sugar   3 eggs
8 tblsp cold water   6 oz sugar
1 pint milk   ½ tsp vanilla essence

Make caramel by putting 4 oz castor sugar and 8 tblsp water in a strong small pan over heat. Stir until sugar is dissolved and continue over heat until it has become a rich golden colour. Do not let it get too dark or it may burn. Line a bowl with the caramel. Whisk the egg whites until stiff and fold in 3 oz of the castor sugar. Fill the caramel-lined bowl ¾ full. Steam very slowly for about 1 hour. Leave in steamer for further hour. Make a custard with the egg yolks. Warm milk and add the remaining sugar and vanilla flavouring, pour over beaten yolks and cook slowly until it coats the back of a wooden spoon. When cool pour over the steamed whites. Turn out to serve. May be made the day before required and kept in fridge.

Time: 2 hrs 30 mins   *Edith McPhail*
Serves 6   *Strathtay*

FLAN VERA CRUZ (MEXICAN CREME CARAMEL)

4 tblsp castor sugar	14 oz sweetened condensed milk
5 oz whipping cream	¼ pint milk
4 egg yolks	1 cinnamon stick (or ground cinnamon)

In a heavy-bottomed frying pan or saucepan stir the sugar carefully until it melts and turns pale golden brown. Spread it quickly over an ovenproof baking dish. Set aside to cool. Mix the other ingredients (except cinnamon) thoroughly and pour onto caramel base. Float the cinnamon stick on top, or sprinkle on the ground cinnamon. Stand the flan in a baking tray containing hot water, and bake in preheated oven at Gas mark 3, 320°F, 160°C, for approximately 50 mins (or until ready!). The flan should be firm, and brownish on the top.

Prep time: 15 mins
Cooking time: 50 mins   *Judith Gonzalez*
Serves 4   *Viva Memco Restaurant, Edinburgh*

HONEY CHEESECAKE

Pastry case:

4 oz flour	3 oz butter
pinch salt	1 egg yolk
milk if needed	

Filling:

6 oz cream cheese	2 oz castor sugar
½ lb cottage cheese	2 oz sesame seeds
1¼ tsp ground cinnamon	5 tblsp honey
3 eggs	

Make shortcrust pastry in the usual way, then roll out, and line a 7½"-8" flan ring or dish. Leave to rest whilst filling is made. Beat the two cheeses together till smooth. Beat in sugar, cinnamon, sesame seeds, honey, and then one at a time, the eggs. Prick over centre of pastry, then pour in the filling. Bake in a hot oven, Gas mark 6, 400°F, 205°C, for 10 mins, then reduce heat at once to slow oven, Gas mark 1, 300°F, 155°C, and bake for about 45 mins longer, when filling should have risen slightly, and be just firm at centre. Turn off heat, and leave in oven with door open to cool slowly, for about ½ hr. When cold, decorate as you fancy.

Prep time: 20 mins
Cooking time: 55 mins
Serves 6-8

Catriona Godson
Chiddingfold

VERY QUICK CHOCOLATE SOUFFLE

1 large tin Carnation milk
2 tblsp Bournville cocoa powder
sugar to taste

1 pkt gelatine powder
2 tblsp Cadbury's drinking
    chocolate powder

Put the tin of Carnation milk in the fridge for 2-3 hours before using. Mix the two chocolate powders in a small quantity of water to make a paste. Dissolve the gelatine in a small quantity of water. Whisk up the milk till stiff, add sugar and the chocolate and gelatine together, continuing to whisk for a few minutes till well blended and pour into a dish for serving. Garnish as required.

Time: 10 mins
Serves 5

Betty Innes
Perth

CHOCOLATE PUDDING, QUICK

2 oz breadcrumbs
4 tblsp chocolate powder
1 chocolate flake

2 oz demerara sugar
½ pint double cream

Mix breadcrumbs (old or new, doesn't matter), sugar and chocolate powder thoroughly, whip cream. Then, in a separate bowl, put in alternate layers of breadcrumb mixture, and cream, finishing with cream on top. Add crumbled flake on top before serving. Sherry can be sprinkled on each layer of mixture, for extra richness.

Time: 10 mins
Serves 6

Ali Constable
Ballintuim

Janetta Watters sent in the same recipe, but hers uses 4 oz breadcrumbs, and 4 oz soft brown sugar to the same ingredients above, and suggests using rum instead of sherry.

Mary Horsfall adds coffee essence to the cream, with no added rum or sherry.

APRICOT AND APPLE MOUSSE

½ lb dried apricots soaked overnight
pared rind and juice of ½ lemon
toasted almonds

2 med cooking apples, peeled,
   cored and sliced
sugar to taste
3 egg whites

Stew apricots gently with lemon rind, juice and apples. Purée in blender or rub through sieve. When cold, sweeten purée to taste. Whip whites stiffly, add by degrees to purée, continuing to whisk. Scatter with toasted almonds or grated chocolate.

Prep time: 30 mins
Serves 6

Jean Rodwell
Blairgowrie

VANILLA SOUFFLE

sponge fingers
10 oz castor sugar
large tin Carnation milk
4 oz double cream

5 standard eggs
vanilla essence
½ oz gelatine

Separate egg whites from yolks. Beat yolks and sugar together until thick and creamy. Mix gelatine with ½ gill water, add to Carnation milk and heat until gelatine is dissolved. Cool. Add vanilla essence. Beat egg whites until stiff and add to mixture. Line a cake tin (loose bottom so that pudding can be pushed out) with sponge fingers, cutting a small piece from bottom of each finger. Fill with souffle mixture and put in fridge to set. Decorate with cream, or as desired.

Time: 25 mins
Serves 8

Mary Rutherford
Coupar Angus

BLACKCURRANT DELIGHT

1 lb blackcurrants
3 level tsp gelatine
3 tblsp cassis (blackcurrant liqueur)
4 oz castor sugar

3 tblsp water
3 egg whites
¼ pint double cream

Cook fruit gently with sugar till pulpy. Sieve to remove pips. Dissolve gelatine in water, in cup over hot water. Stir into fruit purée with cassis. Cool until almost set. Whip the cream till floppy and fold into half set mixture. Whisk egg whites until stiff and fold into the fruit mixture. Spoon into individual glasses and decorate with extra cream.

To freeze: When prepared, place in freezerproof dishes without decoration. When set, wrap, label and freeze. To use, thaw out at room temperature for about 3 hours.

Prep time: 30 mins   *Catriona Godson*
Serves 6   *Chiddingfold*

ORANGE PARFAIT

3 egg whites
8 oz granulated sugar
6½ oz frozen concentrated
   orange juice

pinch of salt
¼ pint water
½ pint whipping cream
1 eggcupful Cointreau (optional)

Whisk egg whites with salt until they stand in soft peaks. In a small saucepan, dissolve the sugar in water over a low heat till melted, and then bring to boil and bubble fiercely for 3 mins. Immediately pour in a thin stream on to the egg whites, whisking all the time. Whisk this until it is like a stiff meringue mixture, then whisk in the orange juice. (This need only be slightly thawed.) Whip cream until thick but not stiff, and stir gently into the meringue mixture. Freeze, preferably overnight.

Prep time: 15 mins (with electric mixer)
No cooking   *Nick Ross*
Serves 4   *BBC TV London*

ICED MERINGUE

4 egg whites
½ pint whipped cream

castor sugar
liqueur or fruit purée

Make meringues with egg whites and sugar. Break them up, add to the whipped cream, which can then be flavoured with any liqueur and frozen – or served (frozen) with any fruit purée.

Prep time: 10 mins
Cooking time: (for meringues) 2 hours   *Sue Sherriff*
Serves 6   *Strathtay*

HONEY AND DRAMBUIE ICE CREAM

8 egg yolks   8 tblsp warmed honey
1 pint double cream   8 tblsp Drambuie

Beat the egg yolks in a warmed Kenwood bowl for about 5 mins until they have expanded as far as possible, then slowly drip in the warmed honey. Carry on beating for a further 5 mins. meanwhile, lightly whip the cream with the Drambuie and then fold the two mixtures together. Pour into ramekin dishes and freeze. This is a soft ice cream which can be served straight from the freezer.

Prep time: 20 mins or less   *Jacqui Brown*
Serves 8   *Kirkmichael*

ELDERFLOWER SORBET

2 egg whites   macaroon biscuits
1 pint water   rind and juice of 3 lemons
6 oz sugar   4 large elderflower heads picked
                                 when dry and at their best

Bring water, sugar and lemon rind to boil, and simmer for 5 mins. Take off heat, plunge elderflowers in and leave to cool. Strain, add lemon juice to liquid and freeze. Whisk whites of eggs stiffly. Remove ice from freezer, whip in whites and refreeze. Repeat process until white and frothy. Serve with small macaroon biscuits.

Time: not long to mix   *Elizabeth Blair*
Serves 6   *Kenmore*

CARAMEL CUSTARD
Cooked in a pressure cooker

3 tblsp sugar   3 tblsp water
1 pint milk   3 eggs
lemon juice   ½ pint water

Make caramel with 3 tblsp water and 3 tblsp sugar. When nicely brown, pour caramel round base and sides of pyrex dish, which will fit in your pressure cooker. Beat eggs, and add to warmed milk. Put ½ pint water in pressure cooker, with a squeeze of lemon juice. Put dish with caramel, into pressure cooker. Pour in egg and milk mixture. Cover with greaseproof paper. Put on lid, and bring to pressure, and cook for 3 mins. Cool slowly, and put in fridge when cold enough.

Prep time: 15 mins
Cooking time: 3 mins   *Diana Dixon*
Serves 4-6   *Louth*

RUSSIAN FRUIT PUDDING

1 lb rasps (or any fruit that's   sugar
   not too juicy   2 eggs
½ pint soured cream   1 tblsp flour

Place fruit in shallow ovenproof dish, and sprinkle with sugar. Warm fruit on middle shelf of oven at Gas mark 2, 300°F, 150°C. Beat up eggs, cream and flour, pour over warmed fruit, and put dish back in same oven, but on top shelf, for about 45 mins. Sprinkle more sugar over top before serving. Good hot or cold.

Prep time: 10 mins
Cooking time: 45 mins   *Barbara Liddell*
Serves 6   *Pitlochry*

QUICK AND EASY ICE CREAM

½ pint whipping cream   2 eggs, separated
2 oz sugar   flavour, to taste

Lightly whip the cream (not too stiffly). Add sugar and whip again. Add flavour and whip again. Add yolks and whip again. Whip whites firm, and fold into mixture. Put into container and freeze. No need to stir whilst freezing. Suggested flavours: 2 capfuls vanilla essence; 2 tsp Camp coffee; purée of passion fruit plus seeds; chocolate, melt 6 oz block chocolate in 4 tblsp water plus 1 tsp coffee. Add when cool.

Prep time: 10 mins
No cooking   *Ruth Hope*
Serves 4-6   *Somerford Keynes*

I envy the male
Who can cook like a dream
I envy his crêpes
And his butterscotch crème
I envy him more,
That he's usually blessed
With an orderly spouse
Who will clean up the mess!

American

Chapter 7

CAKES — BISCUITS — BREAD — JAM & DRINKS

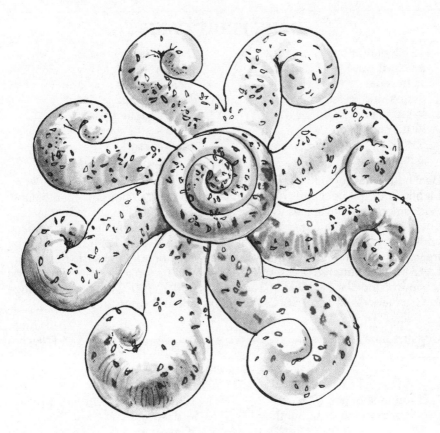

NORTHERN WHEEL

DIGESTIVE BISCUIT CRUST MICROWAVE
(for cheese cakes, flans etc)

Please note: only containers suitable for microwave can be used.

6 oz digestive biscuits
1 oz sugar

2 oz margarine or butter

Melt butter or margarine in pie dish or plate for 1 min only—full power. Add biscuit crumbs and sugar and mix well. Press on to sides and bottom of pie dish or plate. Heat uncovered for 2 mins on full power. Leave to cool.

Prep time: 2 mins
Cooking time: 3 mins

Nighean Ross
Pitlochry

DARK FRUIT CAKE

12 oz plain flour
pinch of salt
½ lb sugar
grated rind ½ lemon
½ tsp mixed spice
¼ tsp cinnamon
5 eggs
2 tblsp treacle

1 tsp baking powder
½ lb butter
½ lb sultanas
½ lb currants
¼ lb chopped peel
¼ lb sliced cherries
½ gill brandy

Beat butter and sugar to a cream. Sieve flour, baking power and salt together. Lightly flour the peel and fruit to prevent it sinking to bottom when baking. Add lemon rind and spices to the creamed butter and mix well. Beat in eggs one at a time alternating eggs with some of the flour, beating well after each addition. Add fruit, but do not beat again, just stir it in. Lastly add warmed treacle, and the brandy. Grease and line a cake tin and pour the mixture in. Lay a piece of buttered greaseproof paper over the top to prevent it browning too much, and place in oven at Gas mark 6, 400°F, 205°C till set, then reduce to Gas mark 4, 340°F, 170°C. It will take about 3 hours in all

Prep time: 15-20 mins
Cooking time: 3 hours

Sheila Keith
Pitlochry

LEMON LAYER CAKE

2 round sponges
  (home made or bought)
4½ oz castor sugar
3 eggs

Roasted sliced almonds to
  decorate
3 ozs butter
rind and juice of 1 lemon

Separate eggs and whip whites. Slice each sponge in 2, or if possible, 3 layers. Beat butter and sugar to a cream and add yolks, juice and rind. Beat well. Fold in stiffly beaten whites. Using a round loose-bottomed tin, lay down alternate layers of sponge and creamed mixture till tin is full. Press down and refrigerate overnight. Turn out, cover with whipped cream and decorate.

Prep time: 15-20 mins   *Hetta McGowan*
No cooking   *Pitlochry*

LEMON DRIZZLE CAKE

6 ozs butter	6 ozs S R flour
6 ozs castor sugar	2 eggs
Rind of lemon, grated	Margarine, for greasing tin

Frosty top:

Juice of lemon   4 ozs granulated sugar

Place all ingredients in bowl and beat with a wooden spoon 2-3 mins, till smooth. Put mixture in tin 12" x 8" x 1" deep, lined with greased proof paper, greased with melted margarine. Bake at Gas mark 4, 370°F, 185°C 15-20 mins. Remove from oven, and whilst hot, mix lemon juice and granulated sugar, and spread over top of sponge. As this cools it becomes frosty and crisp.

Prep time: 10 mins   *Joanna Stephenson*
Cooking time: 20 mins   *Courcheval*

CHERRY & ALMOND CAKE

8 ozs plain flour	8 ozs castor sugar
4 ozs ground almonds	8 ozs margarine
4 ozs cherries halved	pinch salt
½ tsp baking powder	3 eggs

Cream margarine and sugar and add beaten eggs, flour, almonds and cherries—and with last oz of flour, baking powder and salt. Line a swiss roll tin with greaseproof paper, and pour in mixture. Bake at Gas mark 3, 340°F, 170°C for 30 mins, then Gas mark 2, 320°F, 160°C, for 1½ hours. This cake keeps well, and should be kept for a week before using.

Prep time: 10-15 mins   *Frances MacKinnon*
Cooking time: 1½ hours   *Pitlochry*

OLD WIVES' CAKE (YULE CAKE)

1 lb butter
a little grated nutmeg
2 lbs of flour (or as much
as will make a stiff mix)

½ lb castor sugar
1 lb currants

Beat butter to a cream. Mix dry ingredients together and add to creamed mixture. Shape it on a greased paper on an oven sheet and mark with a fork. Bake in cool oven, Gas mark 1, 280°F, 135°C for about 2 or 3 hours. Put a double piece of greased paper round the cake. Keeps in tin for months.

Prep time: 10-15 mins
Cooking time: 2-3 hours

Jennifer Valentine
Aberfeldy

REFRIGERATOR CAKE

½ lb butter
½ lb chocolate
½ lb broken biscuits
2 eggs

2 dessertsp castor sugar
1 tsp Nescafé
½ tsp vanilla

Melt the butter and chocolate, and cool. Add beaten egg and mix well. Break up biscuits into fairly large (size of 5p) pieces, and add to melted ingredients with the sugar, Nescafé and vanilla. Pour into lined cake tin and allow to set in fridge.

Prep time: 15 mins
No cooking
Serves 12

Enid Fenton
Huntingtower

CHOCOLATE KNOBS

3½ ozs each margarine and
vegetable shortening
3 ozs castor sugar
9 ozs plain flour

1 oz cocoa
2½ ozs digestive biscuit crumbs
(approx 5 biscuits)
2 ozs coconut

Beat margarine and vegetable shortening together then beat in castor sugar. Add the sifted flour and cocoa together with the crushed biscuits, gradually.

Put the coconut into a polythene bag. Roll a tsp of the mixture into a ball in your hands and drop it into the bag of coconut; add four or five more balls, then shake them in the bag to coat them. Lay them, with a little space between, on greased trays. Press lightly with a fork.

Bake the knobs in moderate oven, about Gas mark 4 or 350°F, 175°C for about 20 mins. Cool the knobs on a wire tray. Sandwich in pairs with buttercream icing.

Prep time: 15 mins
Cooking time: 20 mins
Makes 20 pairs

Margarite Campbell
Pitlochry

BROWNIES

2 oz from a bar of
   plain chocolate
2 eggs
2 oz plain flour
¼ tsp salt

4 oz butter
8 oz granulated sugar
1 tsp baking powder
4 ozs chopped nuts, optional

Melt chocolate and butter in a small bowl over hot water. Mix all other ingredients, add to chocolate and butter mixture, away from heat. Pour into a well greased and lined tin, 7" x 11". Bake in oven at Gas mark 4, 350°F, 180°C for 30 mins or until a knife inserted in centre comes out cleanly. Do not over cook. Leave mixture in tin for 10 mins to cool and set, then divide into squares and put on a wire cake rack.

Prep time: 10 mins
Cooking time: 30 mins
Makes 15 squares

Barbara Liddell
Pitlochry

FATLESS SPONGE
(Plain or Chocolate)

4 eggs
¼ lb plain flour

½ lb icing sugar
Juice of ½ small lemon

Beat yolks and whites separately, and then together. Beat in icing sugar. Fold in flour and lemon juice. If chocolate cake, use ½ flour and ½ cocoa (2 oz each). Bake in mod oven for ½ hour at Gas mark 4, 370°F, 185°C. Fill with cream or jam or fresh strawberries or peaches. A fool-proof recipe—and good for Aga cookers.

Prep time: 5 mins
Cooking time: 30 mins

Robyn Yellowlees
Perth

CHOCOLATE CAKE

1 rounded tblsp cocoa
4 oz margarine
2 large eggs
1 level tsp baking powder

2 tblsps hot water
4 oz castor sugar
4 oz S R flour

Icing:
1½ oz butter
3 tblsps milk

1 oz cocoa
4 oz icing sugar

Heat the oven to Gas mark 4, 350°F, 180°C. Grease and line an 8″ round cake tin on a foil container. Blend cocoa with the hot water in a large bowl and leave to cool. Add remaining ingredients and beat for 2/3 mins. Turn into tin and bake in oven for 30/40 mins. Turn out and leave to cool.

To make icing, melt the butter in a pan, stir in cocoa, and cook over gentle heat for 1 min. Remove from the heat and add milk and icing sugar. Beat well to mix, and leave to cool until thickened to spreading consistency.

Prep time: 10 mins
Cooking time: 30/40 mins

Catriona Godson
Chiddingfold

MAIDS OF HONOUR

4 oz soft margarine
4 oz ground almonds
2 eggs
4 oz castor sugar
1 oz rice flour

Zest of lemon
Puff or rough puff pastry
  for cases
Raspberry jam

Line small patty tins with thin puff pastry. Place small amount of raspberry jam in the centre. Beat margarine and sugar till light and fluffy, add 1 egg at a time, beating well, then finally the rice flour and almonds and lemon rind. Place a good tsp of filling in each case, and bake in a moderate oven, Gas mark 2, 300°F, 150°C, until nicely brown, about 20 mins. Ground hazelnuts can be substituted for the almonds, then use quince jelly or apricot jam, and spread when cool, with sherry flavoured butter cream and finally dip in ground hazelnuts.

Prep time: 30 mins
Cooking time: 20 mins
Makes 2 doz tarts

Mary Finnie
Pitlochry

CHINESE CHEWS

1 small cup S R flour
½ pkt of dates
¼ lb margarine
7 glacé cherries

½ cup sugar
¾ cup coconut
1 beaten egg (size 4)

Melt margarine slowly. Crumble dates and cut into small pieces. Mix with dry ingredients. Add well beaten egg and mix well. Lastly add margarine. Place in a swiss roll tin lined with greaseproof paper. Spread mixture evenly and score criss cross with a fork. Bake in middle of oven at Gas mark 2, 300°F, 150°C for 25-30 mins. Ready when *not* soft in centre. Cut in squares when cool.

Prep time: 10 mins
Cooking time: 30 mins

Cecilia McLaughlan
Pitlochry

BRIDAL SLICES

4 ozs castor sugar
6 tblsp crushed rich tea biscuits
1 lb currants
¼ lb chopped cherries
Marzipan, Jam.

8 ozs short crust patry
2 oz margarine
1 tsp mixed spice
2 eggs
Royal icing

Line a swiss roll tin with short crust pastry. Cream butter, sugar and eggs well. Add crushed biscuits, spice and fruit and spread over pastry. Cook in oven Gas mark 2, 300°F, 150°C for 45 mins to 1 hour. Cool. Brush with jam, cover with thin layer of marzipan and royal icing. Cut into slices.

Prep time: 10 mins
Cooking time: 1 hour
24 Slices

Jessie Mathieson
Dunkeld

GINGER CUP CAKES

6 tblsp flour
¼ lb margarine
1 tsp ground ginger
½ tsp mixed spice
1 tblsp syrup

2 tblsp brown sugar
1 egg
½ tsp cinnamon
1 tsp baking soda
A little milk

Beat margarine and sugar to a cream. Add egg, syrup, sieved flour and spices, then lastly baking soda mixed with milk. Bake in patty tins at Gas mark 4, 340°F, 170°C for 20 mins.

Prep time: 10 tims
Cooking time: 20 mins
Makes 12-14 cakes

Agnes McDiarmid
Pitlochry

GINGERBREAD (MOIST) I

12 oz plain flour	6 oz soft brown sugar
pinch salt	5 oz margarine
1 rounded tsp ground ginger	4 oz treacle
1 tsp baking powder	4 oz golden syrup
1 tsp baking soda	1 egg
2 oz chopped preserved ginger	⅓ pint milk

Sieve dry ingredients together, stir in preserved ginger. Warm together in pan sugar, fat, treacle and syrup until dissolved (but not hot). Beat egg and add warmed milk to it. Combine all ingredients, mixing to a soft consistency. Pour into greased and lined Yorkshire pudding tin. Bake at Gas mark 3, 340°F, 170°C for about 1½ hours. Turn out on to wire rack. This cake keeps well.

Prep time: 10 mins   *Barbara Brown*
Cooking time: 1½ hours   *Fearnan*

GINGERBREAD II

12 oz plain flour	4 oz margarine
4 oz brown sugar	8 oz treacle
2 tbls ground ginger	2 level tsps soda bicarb
1 egg	¼ pt milk

The following ingredients are not necessary but make good-keeping gingerbread, if added.

2 oz nuts (almonds preferably)	2 oz cherries or
2 oz crystalised ginger	pineapple pieces
4 oz sultanas	

Melt margarine, treacle and sugar in a pan and allow to cool. Sift flour, spices and soda bicarb, stir the treacle mixture and the milk. Mix well and add fruit and nuts. Bake for 1 hour at Gas mark 3, 325°F, 165°C.

Prep time: 15 mins   *Pam McDiarmid*
Cooking time: 1 hour   *Aberfeldy*

DIANA'S GINGERBREAD

12 oz plain flour	6 oz margarine
4 oz sugar	10 oz black treacle
1 gill warm mlik	1 tsp soda bicarb
8 oz sultanas	1 tsp ginger
3 eggs	

Rub in fat, add sugar and treacle, and soda bicarb dissolved in milk, beaten eggs, ginger and sultanas. Mixture should be really sloppy. Put into large greased and lined tin and bake one hour, or longer, at Gas mark 3, 325°F, 165°C.

Undercook. Then place in a tin and don't cut for a few days. This is a real rib-sticker, and goes down extremely well for all sailing or camping weekends.

Prep time: 10-15 mins
Cooking time: 1 hour

Ann Coventry
Abernethy

CHOCOLATE FUDGE BISCUITS

½ lb margarine
6 tblsp cocoa
4 oz sugar

1 lb pkt digestive biscuits
3 or 4 tblsp golden syrup
1 tsp Nescafé

Melt margarine. Add sugar and syrup and bring to the boil. Add cocoa and Nescafé. Mix well. Add crushed biscuits. Add extra margarine if too dry. Spread mixture in greased tin. Put in fridge to set, but cut into slices before it gets too hard!

Makes about 24 slices

Colin Liddell
Pitlochry

CHOCOLATE CHIP BARS

4 oz soft margarine
1 egg
8 ozs S R flour

6 ozs demerara sugar
1 tsp vanilla essence
4 oz chocolate chips

Heat oven to Gas mark 5, 375°F, 190°C – Grease a tin 11" x 7" x 1". Place all ingredients in a bowl and mix thoroughly (easier with hands!) Spread the mixture in the prepared tin and bake 30-40 mins until golden brown, and shrunk from edges of tin. Leave to cool and cut into 16 pieces. A great favourite with the children! Nick, aged 9, makes them on his own.

Prep time: 10 mins
Cooking time: 30-40 mins
Makes 16 pieces

Catriona Godson
Chiddingfold

CHOCOLATE FUDGE TRAY BAKE

3 ozs margarine
1 tblsp cocoa
6 ozs crushed biscuits
4 ozs raisins
8 ozs cooking chocolate

2 ozs sugar
1 beaten egg
2 ozs coconut
2 ozs chopped cherries

Melt margarine and sugar in a heavy based pan. Add cocoa and mix well, remove from heat. Quickly add beaten egg. Return to heat till the mixture reaches simmering point, stirring all the time. Remove from heat, add biscuit crumbs, coconut, raisins and cherries. Mix well together and spread mixture out evenly in a greased swiss roll tin. Cover with melted chocolate.

Prep time: 10 mins   *Ann Duffy*
Serves 16 slices   *Pitlochry*

GINGER SHORTCAKE

For the base:
8 oz margarine or butter
4 oz castor sugar
10 oz plain flour

2 tsp baking powder
1 tsp ground ginger

Cream margarine and sugar and then add dry ingredients and mix well. Press into a large greased swiss roll tin (12" x 8"). Bake at Gas mark 3, 320°F, 160°C for 40 mins.

Topping:
2 oz butter or margarine
3 tsp syrup

4 oz icing sugar
1 tsp ground ginger

Melt butter and syrup in pan, add icing sugar and ginger. Beat until smooth. Pour over *warm* shortcake base. Allow to cool slightly and cut into squares.

Prep time: 5 mins   *Janice Harriman*
Cooking time: 40 mins   *Pitlochry*

CHOCOLATE CRUMBLES

3 Mars bars
3 oz butter or margarine

3 oz Rice Krispies
5 oz plain chocolate

Slice mars bars and melt in double saucepan with margarine. Add Rice Krispies to mixture thoroughly, and press down into oiled baking tins. Melt plain chocolate and pour over mixture. Cool, cut into shapes later on.

Prep time: 10 mins
Cooking time: 5 mins   *Marjory Lady Bonar*
12-18 portions   *Pitlochry*

PRAULINES
(Microwave or Oven)

1 tblsp syrup
4 oz margarine
½ cup sultanas
4 oz cooking chocolate

½ lb crushed digestive biscuits
3 tblsp sugar
3 tblsp cocoa or drinking chocolate

Melt margarine, sugar and syrup in pan (or in microwave 1½ mins). Add cocoa, biscuits, and sultanas—and mix well. Press into a swiss roll tin, until trim – and leave to cool. Melt cooking chocolate over boiling water, in a bowl—(or in microwave, 1-2 mins). Spread over mixture – cut in slices when set. (Any broken biscuits may be used).

Prep time: 10 mins
Makes 25

Catherine Kemp
Blair Atholl

OATCAKES

1 lb medium oatmeal
6 oz fat or dripping
½ teacup cold water

2 handfuls plain flour
1 good tsp sifted salt

Mix oatmeal, flour and salt. Pour melted fat and cold water simultaneously into the middle and mix. Roll between hands into balls the size of a tennis ball. Roll out each ball, in a mixture of flour and oatmeal, approx. ¼ inch thick. Cut into 4. Bake at Gas mark 6, 400°F, 205°C for 20 mins.

Prep time: 5 mins
Cooking time: 20 mins
Makes approx. 24 oatcakes

Mary Stormonth Darling
North Berwick

This recipe came from an old lady in a croft near Inverewe, Wester Ross

STAR BARS

1 cup sugar
1 cup peanut butter
melted chocolate

1 cup syrup
4 cups Rice Krispies

Dissolve sugar and syrup in a pan over low heat. When frothing, add the peanut butter. Put Rice Krispies in a bowl, and when the mixture in the pan has melted, pour it over the Krispies. Mix together and spread over a greased swiss roll tin evenly. Top with melted chocolate and allow to set.

When cold, cut into squares.

Cooking time: 15 mins

Vivien Rossaak
Johannesburg

REFRIGERATOR BISCUITS

1 cup sugar
1 egg
1¾ cup plain flour
¼ tsp salt
½ cup nuts (optional)

½ cup butter
1 tsp vanilla essence
or ½ tsp grated lemon rind
1½ tsp baking powder
Demerara sugar

Beat butter and sugar till creamy, beat in the egg, and add vanilla or lemon rind. Sift flour with salt and baking powder and stir into butter mixture. Add nuts if liked. Make into a long roll about 2" in diameter. If dough is too soft to handle chill first. When fairly firm, roll the roll in demerara sugar or ground nuts, re-chill rolled in greaseproof paper. Put in fridge for 24 hours before cooking, the dough freezes well at this stage, or will keep up to a week in fridge. When required, slice very thinly and bake on a greased sheet in oven at Gas mark 6, 400°F, 205°C, for about 10 mins. Replace in fridge any dough not used.

Prep time: 10 mins
Cooking time: 10 mins
Makes about 40 biscuits

Barbara Liddell
Pitlochry

NUTTY SLICES

Base:
4 oz butter or hard margarine
1 oz light soft brown sugar
4 oz plain flour

Filling:
6 oz light soft brown sugar
2 eggs
2 oz walnut pieces
5 oz desiccated coconut
2 tblsp Roses lime juice

Icing:
8 oz icing sugar
Roses lime juice
Green food colouring

11" x 7" swiss roll tin, greased

Rub butter (base ingredients) into flour and sugar, when like breadcrumbs, knead together in a bowl and then press into base of tin. Bake at Gas mark 5, 375°F, 190°C, for 15 mins. Meanwhile, mix filling: mix all ingredients together ready to spread over base when it comes out of oven. Bake a further 25-30 mins till golden. Cool in tin. Blend the sieved icing sugar with enough lime juice to make a smooth coating consistency. Add a little colouring, then coat the mixture in the tin and leave till set. Cut into 24 finger shaped slices.

Prep time: 10 mins
Cooking time: 45 mins *Vivien Rossaak*
Makes 24 slices *Johannesburg*

JOANNA'S BISCUITS

6 oz margarine
1 tsp soda bicarb
4 ozs plain flour
6 ozs castor sugar

1 tblsp golden syrup
2 tblsp water
5 ozs quaker oats

Melt margarine and syrup in pan. Dissolve bicarb in water and add to pan. Mix flour, oats and sugar. Pour on liquid and mix well. Place in spoonfuls on greased baking sheet allowing room for them to spread. Bake in oven Gas mark 2, 300°F, 150°C for 15-20 mins. Cool on wire rack.

Prep time: 10 mins *Joanna Stephenson*
Cooking time: 15-20 mins *Courcheval*

RAISIN BISCUITS

4 ozs butter
1 cup sultanas
1 cup S R flour

¾ cup sugar
1 egg
cornflakes

Cream butter and sugar, add egg and beat well. Fold in the sifted flour alternately with the fruit. Roll in cornflakes, 1 tsp full makes a reasonable sized biscuit. (It will flatten itself in the oven). Cook for 10-15 mins, or until lightly browned, at Gas mark 4, 340°F, 170°C. Cook on wire rack.

Prep time: 30 mins *Jill Usher*
Makes about 25-30 biscuits *Christchurch, N.Z.*

NORTHERN WHEEL
(As illustrated)

For the starter dough (make the previous day)

2 tblsp milk	4 tblsp water
1 tsp oil	1 tsp dried yeast
2 tblsp lukewarm water	1 tsp castor sugar
2 tsp salt	4 ozs strong plain flour

Combine the milk, 2 tblsp of cold water and the oil in a saucepan and bring to the boil. Allow to cool until lukewarm. Blend the yeast with 1 tblsp lukewarm water, with the sugar and leave for 5 mins. Add to the milk mixture with the salt. Stir this liquid into the flour until well blended, then cover and leave to stand for 12-18 hours.

2 lbs light rye flour	¾ oz fresh yeast
1½ pints lukewarm water	2 tsp salt
2 tsp caraway seeds	2 tsp dried fennel
2 tsp ground aniseed	Milk to glaze

Place half the flour in a mixing bowl, cream the yeast with a little of the lukewarm water, add the remaining water and mix thoroughly into the flour, together with the starter dough. Knead until smooth, cover and leave to stand in a warm place overnight. Preheat the oven to very hot, Gas mark 8, 450°F, 230°C. Mix the salt, half the spices and the rest of the flour into the dough until smooth. Form ⅓ of the dough into a long roll. Roll up to resemble a snail's shell and place in the middle of a large floured baking tray. Form the remaining dough into 8 rolls 8" in length and place around the central coil and slightly roll the end of each piece as illustrated. Brush the surface of the bread with milk, and sprinkle with the rest of the spices. Bake for 25 mins in pre-heated oven, as above, until golden brown. This loaf was enormous fun to draw but I would never dream of actually making anything so complicated. However for those ambitious cooks, inspired by the illustration and with 2 days to spare – here it is for you.

Time: 2 days   *Maggie Thorburn*
                                                       Enochdhu

NUTTY WHOLEMEAL BREAD

2 ozs cracked wheat
2 ozs sunflower seeds
1¼ lbs wholemeal brown flour
12 ozs water – (half boiling,
  ½ cold, mixed)
1 tsp salt

1 dessertsp castor sugar, or
  soft brown
1½ oz lard
1 packed Golden Harvest yeast

Mix all dry ingredients. Rub in fat, then add yeast granules, sugar and salt. Mix well, and then add water. Knead slightly, cover with oiled paper and leave to rise till double in size. Remove from bowl when well risen, knead again for a short time, shape, and place in well greased bread tin, cover again with oiled paper, and when risen just above rim of tin, bake in a hot pre-heated oven Gas mark 7, 440°F, 225°C for 45 mins – cool on rack.

Prep time: 15 mins plus rising time
Makes 1 loaf
Cooking time: 45 mins

Barbara Liddell
Pitlochry

HARVO LOAF

3 cups S R flour
2 tblsp syrup or treacle
1 cup raisins

¾ cup sugar
1½ cups milk

Mix dry ingredients, then add warmed syrup or treacle, and milk. Mix well and bake in a greased loaf tin for about 1 hour in a slow oven, Gas mark 2, 320°F, 160°C.

Prep time: 5 mins
Cooking time: 1 hour

Sybil Currie
Moulin

HERB SODA LOAF

1 lb plain flour or brown wholewheat
1 tsp salt
2 tsps cream of tartar
2 tblsp freshly cut herbs, such as
  mint, parsley, chives, sage and fennel
  chopped in a parsley mill

2 tsp bicarb-soda
8 ozs warm sour milk

Place all dry ingredients in a bowl. Make a well in the centre and pour in the milk to make a soft dough. Add extra warm sour milk if necessary. Shape with floured hands on a well dredged board into a round flattish cake. Bake at once on a floured sheet in the oven at Gas mark 7, 400°F, 205°C for 40 mins.

Prep time: 5 mins
Cooking time: 40 mins

Mary Horsfall
Kinloch Rannoch

YOGHOURT BREAD

4 cups nutty wheat flour
1 heaped tsp salt
1 heaped tsp bicarb soda

500 ml yoghourt
2 tblsp run honey

Mix all ingredients together, bake at Gas mark 6, 400°F, 205°C, for 20 mins, then Gas mark 7, 425°F, 210°C, for 40 mins.

Prep time: 5 mins
Cooking time: 60 mins

Teddy Matthews
Port Elizabeth, S.A.

BRAN BREAD

2 oz bran
2 oz brown sugar

2½ oz S R flour
¼ pint milk

Mix all dry ingredients and add milk. Put into a greased loaf tin and bake for 45 mins in the oven at Gas mark 4, 350°F, 175°C.

Prep time: 3 mins
Cooking time: 45 mins
Makes 1 small loaf

Edith Martin
Calvine

BOURNVITA LOAF

8 oz S R flour
2 tblsp sugar
1 tblsp warm syrup
2 oz Bournvita

4 oz dried fruit – any, but nice
  to have some glacé cherries
milk to mix

Mix all together, add milk to a dropping consistency. Bake at Gas mark 5, 375°F, 190°C for about 45 mins, in a tin which has been lined with greaseproof paper. Eat hot or cold, buttered or plain.

Prep time: 10 mins
Cooking time: 45 mins

Mary Horsfall
Kinloch Rannoch

BROWN LOAF (NO YEAST)

2 cups Allinson's whole wheat plain flour
2 cups S R flour
2 cups milk
1 small tsp salt

1 tblsp syrup
1 small tsp soda bicarb
1 small tsp cream of tartar

Mix all ingredients together. Bake for 55 mins in greased bread tin, at Gas mark 4, 350°F, 175°C.

Prep time: 5 mins
Cooking time: 55 mins

Jean Simpson
Strathtay

LINDA'S FRUIT LOAF

1 cup cold tea
1 lb mixed fruit

1 cup soft brown sugar
2 cups S R flour

Steep tea, sugar and fruit and leave overnight. Next day add S R flour and mix well. Bake in mod oven Gas mark 4, 340°F, 170°C for 1½ hours in a well greased loaf tin.

Prep time: Overnight steeping + 5 mins
Cooking time: 1½ hours

Helen Benzies
Meigle

LUCY'S FRUIT LOAF

1 lb fruit (sultanas, etc.)
12 oz brown sugar
¾ pint water
12 oz wholemeal flour

1 tsp mixed spice
2 oz butter
1 tsp cinnamon
2 tsp baking powder

Dissolve all ingredients except flour and baking powder, in a pan. Boil for 5 mins and cool. Then mix in when cool, flour and baking powder. Bake in oven, Gas mark 4, 350°F, 175°C for 1¼ to 1½ hours. This keeps remarkably well.

Prep time: 15 mins
Cooking time 1¼ to 1½ hours

Mary Finnie
Pitlochry

MALT FRUIT LOAF

2 dessertsp syrup
2 dessertsp malt
4 ozs dried fruit
½ to 1 cup milk

2 dessertsp treacle
8 oz S R flour
1 dessertsp sugar

Melt syrup, treacle and malt in pan. Add dry ingredients and mix well. Add enough milk to make a fairly heavy consistency. Bake in a lined 2 lb tin for one hour at Gas mark 4, 350°F, 175°C.

Prep time: 15 mins
Cooking time: 1 hour

Gail Fawcus
Aviemore

BISHOP'S BREAD (TYROLEAN)

4 eggs and their weight in icing sugar   6 ozs flour
2 ozs plain chocolate   1 oz chopped almonds
2 ozs raisins or currants   Angelica, a few dates
4 or 5 glace cherries   Juice and rind of 1/2 lemon

Chop chocolate into small lumps, slice cherries and chop dates. Wash raisins and thoroughly dry them. Mix together chocolate, dates, chopped almonds, sliced angelica, cherries and raisins. Sift the flour. Separate the yolks and whites of eggs. Set aside 2 tblsps of icing sugar. Whisk together the egg yolks, lemon juice and remaining sugar, until white and thick. The mixture will be stiff at first and you may have to stir it before you whisk it. Whip the egg whites till stiff, with a pinch of salt added, then whisk in the 2 tblsps sugar. Fold the whipped egg whites into the yolk mixture, alternately with the flour. Finally add the fruit mixture, dry ingredients and grated lemon rind. Bake for 35-40 mins at Gas mark 4, 360°F, 180°C in a buttered and floured rectangular cake tin. Dust with icing sugar while still hot, and set aside to cool on a wire tray. Eat in slices, with butter.

Prep time: 15 mins   *George Cameron*
Cooking time 35-40 mins   *Boat of Garten*

COLD TEA LOAF

1½ lbs dried fruit   ½ lb demerara
¾ pt strained cold tea   1 lb S R flour
1 egg   Pinch of salt

Soak the dried fruit and sugar in the cold tea overnight. Next day stir in the flour, salt and well beaten egg. Divide the mixture between two 2 lb greased loaf tins and bake in a mod. oven, Gas mark 4, 360°F, 180°C for 1-1½ hours. (A wartime recipe – 40 years old)

Prep time: 10 mins plus overnight soaking   *Joyce Heller*
Cooking time: 1-1½ hours   *Edinburgh*

CHERRY BREAD

¾ cup castor sugar   2 cups flour
1 egg well beaten   ½ cup walnuts
1 small jar cherries and juice   2 tsp baking powder
¼ tsp salt (or less)   2 tblsp melted butter

Cream butter, egg and sugar. Drain juice from cherries and add to milk to make 1 cup of liquid. Add to 1st mixture. Sift in flour, baking powder, salt and walnuts and cherries last. Bake for 1 hour at Gas mark 3, 325°F, 165°C.

Prep time: 10 mins   *Lily Donald*
Cooking time: 1 hour   *Pitlochry*

MARMALADE

2½ lbs Seville oranges	½ lb lemons
6 lbs preserving sugar	3 pints water

Scrub fruit well. Put in pressure cooker whole, with the water. When steam escapes steadily from vent, put on 10 lb pressure weight, bring to pressure, and cook for 20 minutes. Do not open for 10 minutes until pressure has reduced. If you have no pressure cooker you can boil the fruit whole in a lidded pan till soft. When fruit is cold, reserve juice, cut fruit in quarters, remove and discard pips, and either slice by hand, or chop in liquidiser, using all flesh of orange as well. Make up the liquid the fruit was cooked in, to 3 pints. At this stage you can put cut fruit and measured liquid into an ice cream polythene box and freeze it. This way you can have freshly made marmalade throughout the year. Each boiling of the above quantities makes 12 lbs of marmalade, so you can work out how many boilings you need to keep you in marmalade for 12 months. Thaw completely and continue as follows:—

Warm the sugar and the jars in the oven. Boil peel and juices hard for 15-20 mins testing for setting after 15 mins. Allow the marmalade to cool in the pan for at least 10 mins before putting in pots, to prevent the peel from rising to the top, then pot and cover immediately.

The marmalade recipe came from Dr Rosamund Gruer, Edinburgh. The deep freezing is my idea, having been caught out with no sugar in the house or shops the year there was a lorry strike, and I've done it that way ever since.

Time: 40 mins plus cutting up time *Barbara Liddell*
Makes 12 x 1 lb jars *Pitlochry*

STRAWBERRY JAM (NEVER FAIL)

Equal amounts of fruit and sugar.

Put strawberries and sugar in layers in a large bowl. Leave for 24 hours. Place in preserving pan and boil for 5 mins. Return to bowl and leave for 48 hours. Place in preserving pan again and boil for 10-20 mins until set. Cool, stir and pour into pots. It should cool well or the strawberries will rise to the top.

Prep time: 24 hours + 48 hours *Jean Robertson*
Cooking time: 20 mins *Dunkeld*

DRIED APRICOT JAM

1 lb dried apricots	juice of 1 lemon
3 lbs sugar	3½ pints boiling water

Wash apricots, pour over 3½ pints boiling water. Leave overnight to soak. Boil till tender (about 1 hour).

Add sugar and boil till it jellies on a plate, put in jars. Label when cool. The jam will take approx ½ hour to set, and these ingredients will make about 6 lbs of jam.

Prep time: 5 mins + overnight soak
Cooking time: 1 hour

Mary Horsfall
Kinloch Rannoch

LEMON – WINE DRINK

One-third fizzy lemonade
One-third white wine
One-third fruit juice (orange of lemon etc.)

Mix all together, service chilled
Good for young teenagers

Jill Usher
Christchurch, N.Z.

MULLED CIDER

2 oz light brown sugar	4 whole cloves
3 whole allspice crushed	2 quarts cider
3 one inch pieces cinnamon stick	Pinch of salt
A good grating of nutmeg	

Put sugar, allspice, cloves, cinnamon, nutmeg, salt and cider into a large saucepan, and simmer for 10 mins. Serve hot, strained.

Makes about 1½ pints

Barbara Liddell
Pitlochry

MULLED CLARET

1 quart Claret
½ banana
1 stick cinnamon
1 cup rum

4 oz sugar candy
4 cloves
1 sliced lemon

Put Claret in an enamel pan on stove and heat almost to boiling point. Tie candy, cinnamon, cloves, banana and lemon in a piece of cheesecloth. Put into hot claret. Let it mull on back of stove for ½ an hour. Serve very hot.

Barbara Liddell
Pitlochry

Makes about 1½ pints

PARSLEY WINE

1 lb French parsley
4 lbs sugar
2 oranges

1 gall water
2 lemons
½ oz yeast

Pour 1 gallon boiling water onto 1 lb of parsley, and leave for 24 hrs. Strain through muslin and boil the liquid with rind of oranges and lemons for 20 mins. Put 4 lbs sugar into a bowl or crock, and strain the boiled liquid into it, stirring until sugar dissolves. Add juice of fruit. When cool, add ½ oz yeast, previously dissolved in liquid. Leave in warm place, (stirring occasionally) for 5 days, until fermentation has subsided and the wine is clear. This takes about 2 months. Draw off into bottles. It is better to make a large quantity at a time (say 5 galls), as small quantities do not ferment so well.

This is delicious, keeps well, and is quite potent!

Barbara Liddell
Pitlochry

If it's loose, pick it up
If it isn't, dust it
If it moves, feed it

American

Chapter 8

HOUSEHOLD HINTS

1. **Gelatine** is easily prepared in the Microwave. Place gelatine and water in a cup and heat for approx. 30 seconds to dissolve the grains. DO NOT BOIL.

   Nighean Ross
   Pitlochry

2. **Gelatine** is also easily prepared in the Magimix. Put gelatine and boiling water into Magimix bowl. Switch on and process until metled. Ratio of 1½ tsps gelatine to 4 tblsps boiling water.

   Barbara Liddell
   Pitlochry

3. **Burnt casseroles and pans** – Soak them in Ariel overnight. Everything should come off next morning, quite easily.

   Ann Common
   Fortingall

4. **Stains on enamel bath** may be removed by making a paste from hydrogen peroxide and cream of tartar. Leave on for a few hours and then rinse well.

   Anon

5. **To sour cream** – Add 1 tsp lemon juice or 5 fl oz single or double cream. Leave for half an hour and it will thicken and become sour. A quicker method is to mix equal quantities of cream and plain yoghurt.

   Barbara Liddell
   Pitlochry

6. **To cure Migraine** – Eat one or two leaves per day of chrysanthemum, partheneum or common feverfew, in a sandwich of bread and butter or biscuit. After 3 months even frequent and bad migraines will be less severe. After 6 months they should be cured completely. It is advisable to continue the treatment after cure to ensure that the migraines don't start again. It is difficult to keep plants growing in the winter, even in a greenhouse, but feverfew pills are obtainable from health shops.

   Barbara Liddell
   Pitlochry

7. **Carpet and mattress stains** – Spray soda water at once on dogs' puddles, stained mattresses and rub dry.

   Anne Howell
   Pitlochry

8. **To clean linoleum or vinyl** – Use a little Brasso on a clean cloth and wipe off.

   Pamela Carmichael
   Meigle

9. **Silver** – Clean properly, in your usual way, and store with a few cubes of block camphor. This can be bought from most chemists, who can order it if it is not in stock. The cubes will eventually disappear and must be replaced. However the silver will remain untarnished and can be taken into use with only the lightest of rubs with a silver cloth. It is not even necessary to put the silver into bags, though a cloth over the top to keep off the dust is advisable.

Edward Aglen
Edinburgh

10. **Soap ends** – Save scraps of soap of all kinds. Put in large jam jar and cover with boiling water. Stir well so that they all dissolve and mix. This mixture can then be used to fill an empty soap dispenser and perfume can be added if liked.

Jean Scott
Pitlochry

11. **Loo Cleaner** – Use a polythene house or greenhouse hand sprayer. Fill with disinfectant according to strength recommended on bottle and use to spray loo inside and out. Rub with a wet cloth and then a dry one.

Jean Scott
Pitlochry

12. When **rinsing any silk articles,** add a few drops of methylated spirits in the final rinse, mixing well before adding the silk. It helps to stiffen the silk when ironing while damp.

Enid Fenton
Huntingtower

13. **Honey** – To obtain run honey from a jar of honey which has become solid, place jar on a saucer with lid removed, and heat gently in a low oven until clear and liquid. It should stay liquid, but if it does thicken just heat gently again.

Barbara Liddell
Pitlochry

14. **To remove gum** and adhesive tape from clothing use lemon juice or a cube of ice.

Anon

15. **When painting** woodwork round winows, wet newspapers and stick to glass.

Anon

16. **To remove iron marks** from linen, rub with lemon juice and salt.

Anon

17. To preserve the **fresh colour of bananas** for a fruit salad, etc. soak the whole banana, skin and all, in cold water the night before required. The skin will go black, but the banana will look fresh inside and can be sliced or mashed and will not lose its colour.

Iris Colin
Louth

18. **Mayonnaise, Bernaise or Hollandaise sauce** which curdles can be rescued by adding 1 ice cube to mixture. Whisk again and all should be well.

Elizabeth Blair
Kenmore

19. **Sponge Cakes** will rise better if sugar is heated in oven while eggs are being whipped, and added warm to the partially whipped eggs.

Meg Fergusson
Pitlochry

20. **Fruit stained hands** can be avoided when handling fresh fruit, by rubbing lemon juice on your hands and allowing it to dry first.

Meg Fergusson
Pitlochry

21. **Meringues** – These whip much better if the eggs have been kept in the fridge for 36 hours before being used.

Betty Innes
Perth

22. **Brass & Copper cleaner** – POISON – so label well.

 ½ oz oxalic acid (bought from chemist)
 ½ pt warm water

Mix and bottle.

Damp a small cloth with mixture and rub on brass and copper. Polish with a dry cloth. Repeat if badly tarnished. Cheap and effective, but wear rubber gloves.

Beryl Bateman
London

23. **Lumpy soft brown sugar** – To remove lumps put in fridge overnight.

Clodagh Bonham-Carter
Comrie

24. **New potatoes** – To bring out the flavour of new potatoes boil them in the usual way, but do not add the mint until they are nearly cooked. Pour away all the water, add the mint, replace saucepan lid and leave for about 5 minutes.

Rosalind Stewart-Wilson
Moulin

25. **Jam and marmalade** – To avoid mould when making jam or marmalade, with used-before metal tops for covering jars, boil tops for 15 minutes immediately before using, and dry if necessary with kitchen paper. Cover jam as soon as possible, while still warm, to avoid any mould spores entering.

Lady Balfour of Burleigh
Brucefield

26. **To stabilise yoghurt** – In order that yoghurt doesn't curdle in cooking, it needs to be stabilised. To do this you need to add either 1 egg white to 2 pints yoghurt, or 1 tblsp of cornflour, mixed with a little cold water or milk.

Method: Beat yoghurt in a large saucepan until liquid. Add egg white, or cornflour mixture, and add a little salt. Stir well with a wooden spoon *in one direction only.* Bring to boil slowly, stirring constantly, always in the same direction, then reduce heat to as low as possible and let yoghurt barely simmer, *uncovered,* for about 10 minutes, or until has has a thick rich consistency. *Do not cover pan,* since a drop of steam falling back into the yoghurt could spoil it. After simmering, the yoghurt can be mixed and cooked with other ingredients such as meat and vegetables, with no danger of curdling.

Barbara Liddell
Pitlochry

27. **Ginger remedy for dizziness** –

    1 to 4 slices fresh ginger, cut very thin
    1 heaped tsp dark brown soft sugar
    1 glass water

Heat ingredients in a small saucepan, simmer for 4 or 5 minutes, strain and drink hot. This is very good for head colds also. Drink last thing at night or whenever necessary.

Helen Nairn
Pitcarmick

INDEX

VOLUME & LIQUID MEASUREMENTS
(recommended measurements)

1 level tsp = 5ml
1 level dessertsp = 10ml
1 level tblsp = 15ml

(ML) = Millilitres

Ounces and Fluid ozs	Grammes & ML	Decilitres	Cups
1	25 (to nearest unit of 25)		
2	50		
3	75		
4	100		
5 (¼ pt) 1 gill	150	1.5	
6	175		
7	200		
8 (¼ lb)	225		
9	250		1
10 (½ pt)	275	3	
11	300		
12	350		
13	375		1½
14	400		
15 (¾ pt)	425	4.5	
16 (1 lb)	450		
17	475		
18	500		2
19	550		
20 (1 pt)	575	6	
2 lbs 3 ozs	1 kilogram		
1¾ pints	1 litre	10	4

CONVERSION TABLES
OVEN TEMPERATURE

	Degrees Fahrenheit	Gas Regulo	Degrees Centigrade
Very Slow	240-280	¼-½	115-135
Slow	280-320	1	135-160
Warm	320-340	3	160-170
Moderate	340-370	4	170-185
Fairly Hot	370-400	5-6	185-205
Hot	400-440	7	205-225
Very Hot	440-500	8-9	225-250

Standard measuring cup	=	½ pint
¼ cup liquid	=	3 tblsp
½ cup liquid	=	1 gill
½ cup butter = 1 stick	=	¼ lb
2 cups butter	=	1 lb
2 cups grated cheese	=	½ lb approx
5 cups grated cheese	=	1 lb
2 cups cottage cheese	=	1 lb
2 level tblsp flour	=	1 oz
4 cups flour	=	1 lb
2 cups raw rice	=	1 lb
1 level tblsp white sugar	=	1 oz
2 cups granulated or castor sugar	=	1 lb
2 cups firmly packed brown sugar	=	1 lb
2 large eggs	=	3 small eggs
1 average lemon	=	3-4 tblsp juice
1 average orange	=	6-8 tblsp juice
Granted peel of 1 orange	=	1 tblsp
1 lb ground coffee	=	80 tblsp